The Feel Good Food Guide

Making the pH connection be
foods and common alle

by Deborah Page Johnson, B.F.A.

Formerly published as —

The Feel Good Food Guide:
Easy Recipes Free of Sugar, Wheat, Yeast, Corn, Eggs, Dairy & Soy!

ISBN -13: 978-0-9652484-2-6
ISBN -10: 0-9652484-2-9

Fifth Edition, July 2006
Fourth Edition, March 2001
Third Edition, September 1999
Second Edition, August 1997
First Edition, October 1996

Book and cover design by DMJ Design & Advertising
Cover photograph by Robert Smith

Printed: Sioux Printing, Inc.
500 East 52nd Street North
Sioux Falls, SD 57104-0639
U.S.A.

Important Notice

The author and publisher assume no responsibility for any health effects or result obtained from utilizing the information in this book.

Many different views and foods are represented in this book. Without knowing an individual's particular health history, it is impossible to know if an allergic reaction may occur to any foods. Caution is advised if you are not sure of the outcome. Even alternative foods can cause an allergic reaction.

The information provided herein should not be used during any medical emergency or for the diagnosis or treatment of any and all medical conditions. The information is provided for educational purposes only, and is not advice or prescription.

This book is intended to be used in conjunction with the guidance of your health-care professional. If you have, or think you have, a medical problem, seek qualified professional help immediately.

Do not stop taking medication without consulting your doctor first.

The statements and information contained in this book have not been evaluated by the FDA. In the event that you use this information on your own, know you are prescribing for yourself (this is your Constitutional right).

NewPage™ Productions, Inc.
1910 S. Highland Avenue • Suite 250
Lombard, IL 60148
www.feelgoodfood.com

Testimonials & Acknowledgements

"Debbie, thanks so much for your support and wonderful efforts to bring nutritional consciousness to humanity. Best wishes always, God bless!"
– Leonard G. Horowitz, D.M.D., M.A., M.P.H. Author of Emerging Viruses

– Joseph Keon Ph.D., has listed The Feel Good Food Guide as a reference in his self-help book: Truth About Breast Cancer: A 7-Step Prevention Plan. Dr. Keon brings light to the importance of a clean diet in the prevention of cancer.

– Shelly Redford Young is the premiere authority on the Alkalarian approach to good health. Mrs. Young has included Spicy Kale Slaw by Deborah Page Johnson in her cook book: Back to the House of Health 2.

– Myryam Ehrlich Williamson is using feelgoodfood.com as a reference for her latest book. Myryam won an American Medical Writers Association Will Solimene Award for: Excellence in Medical Communication for Fibromyalgia: A Comprehensive Approach. She is a technical journalist and a charter member of the on-line Fibromyalgia Discussion Group.

"Please pass along to Debbie that her book has been a God-send for us! We use the book regularly and have found it to be the most useful of the many I have purchased. Job well done!!!"
– Jennifer Irby

Food for People with Food Allergies... "finally brownies without hives"
– Editorial Review - Chicago Daily Herald

"A big thank you to Deborah and everyone at feelgoodfood.com. Incredible information! Many blessings & with deep gratitude."
– Janine Nugent, Sierra Childbirth Institute

"I think most people would be shocked. You really don't have to give up "taste" to eat healthy! I really enjoyed the Spinach Bake out of The Feel Good Food Guide. Ryann seems to be much better! Thanks again! We really appreciate it!"
– Jodie Holden

"Her (Deborah Page Johnson) book is filled with timeless recipes that promote healthy eating and adapt beautifully to rotation diets."
– Betsy Hicks, Diet Counselor, Pathways Medical Advocates

"This is one of the most important books in the health field today for those people who have allergies, health challenges and are in need of pH balancing. But also an exceptional book for those people just wanting to increase their nutrition and dynamic health. I whole heartedly recommend this book to my clients and anyone trying to do a better job with food choices. It solves the problem – what is there to eat?"
– Sybil E. Wander, B.A., C.N.C.

Dedication

This book is dedicated to the ones I love.

My husband, partner, best friend, co-worker (and sometimes antagonist) Dave Johnson who has selflessly shared my desire to help the human condition. His artistic genius has helped me present my ideas and philosophy in a visually beautiful and appealing way. His support in every way imaginable is never forgotten and is always appreciated by myself and everyone who has ever visited our website, purchased a book, product or found useful the ideas we have presented. Thank you Dave, for always keeping me on track and focused on the big picture.

For my sons Christopher and Zachary, the loves of my life. My mother Rose Page for teaching me the love of vegetables and good food. My father Earl for teaching me that I can do anything. All of my friends, especially Sybil who's support has been invaluable.

I am additionally grateful for the gift of the past ten years and the people who have personally and through their work come into my life. I honor the work of the men and women, both past and present, who have dedicated their God given talents to shedding light on the basic chemistry of life. Whether we choose to believe it or not, the truth is the truth and needs no defense. I dedicate this book to each and every human being on this planet seeking better health for themselves and for the people they care for. Love of life and a peaceful existence for spaceship earth and all of its inhabitants is a goal for which I strive every day.

Table of Contents

Forward

I remember the first time I spoke to Deborah. I was a mother of an extremely ill little boy looking to food for answers as help through traditional medicine had completely failed.

She was one of the first people who helped me re-think diet and medicine, preparing me for a career in writing, lecturing and radio. I think of foods that I speak about each day now in my career, words like quinoa (Keen-Wah) and amaranth (Am-a-Ranth) that Deborah taught me how to use and how to pronounce. Deborah's ability to create recipes with so few incriminating ingredients has stuck with me over the decade, and her original lessons to me are still the ones I use to now teach others.

Her book is filled with timeless recipes that promote healthy eating and adapt beautifully to rotation diets.

Betsy Hicks
Diet Counselor, Pathways Medical Advocates

LET YOUR FOOD BE YOUR MEDICINE AND
LET YOUR MEDICINE BE YOUR FOOD!

HIPPOCRATES,
THE FATHER OF MODERN MEDICINE

Preface

When I first published The Feel Good Food Guide: Easy Recipes Free of Sugar, Wheat, Yeast, Corn, Eggs, Dairy and Soy! ten years ago, . . . I had no idea that the foods and chemicals my family was allergic to were also highly acid-forming. It wasn't until I started researching pH information for the Home Test pH Kit that I realized the connection. Everything we were allergic or sensitive to was also acidic. Wow, could it be possible that these highly allergic foods and products simply had never been a good idea to eat and use? We now follow the 80% - 20% rule. Simply put, eighty percent of our diet consists of alkaline-forming raw organic (when possible) vegetables and twenty percent healthy acid-forming foods such as whole grains, nuts, seeds and small wild caught fish (with scales, no shellfish or smooth skinned fish). I avoid most of the traditional grains. Sprouting changes the grain bio-chemically from a grain to a plant. There is an energy in a sprout that exponentially increases its nutritional qualities. Once a plant grain becomes alkalizing and can be tolerated by most. There is no gluten in wheat grass. Gluten is only found in the grain. However, if you are gluten intolerant, or have a known allergy, check with your doctor first and make sure. Ask questions rather than suffer the consequences of a poor choice.

Fifteen years ago when I walked into my first health food store, . . . I had no idea where the journey would lead. The "new" information I was learning has been around for thousands of years. Why had I not heard it before? It just felt like basic common sense to me. I have found that when people truly "get it" this is highly contagious information. Humans have this in-born need to share. The information flowed out of my need to channel the rage inside of me in a positive way. The dream of a healthy happy society slips further away from us every time a new child becomes part of the epidemic of autism, obesity, heart disease, diabetes and learning disabilities that are plaguing our modern world.

I have redesigned this book to address the new information and have changed the subtitle to reflect the change. It is now The Feel Good Food Guide: Making the pH connection between acid-forming foods and common allergenic foods. I have removed a few recipes and added others. Most importantly, we have included pH information to show the connection. Little did I know ten years ago that I was writing what would become a transitional recipe guide for food and life. This book is filled with "healthier alternatives" for some old comfort food favorites. Just as we place training wheels on a bicycle to learn balance, we need to do the same with diet, thought, exercise and health care. I guarantee, once you experience balance, you will never forget how you feel and you will never want to be out of balance again.

I can not say enough about the importance of balanced pH levels in the tissues of our body. If not balanced, acid pH levels can have a negative effect on our health. As I stated earlier, over the years I have observed that most allergenic/sensitive foods and beverages are also the highly acid foods. The cells of our body are acid. In order for life to carry on, the cells must do their job in an alkaline medium, our blood. This acid function, taking place in an alkaline medium, creates energy or, in other words, is the spark of life itself. If we are not giving our body the alkaline fuel it needs in the way of fresh green vegetables, our body must look to bone and tissue for the alkalizing minerals it needs to survive.

Preface

Choosing a diet rich in brightly colored vegetables is gaining popularity among health conscious individuals everywhere for a reason. Balancing the pH levels within your body is the cornerstone for recovery from a candida overgrowth, food sensitivities, acid reflux and is linked to many other health concerns.

No one and no magic pill can heal us. And if anyone says they can, run as fast as you can. There are of course medical and wellness professionals who can assist with the healing process and have effective treatments for crisis situations. Let me be the first to say I am grateful that they are there. However, it is the daily choices we make when fueling our body that create the opportunity for wellness. Our body knows how to heal itself. We can only assist by giving it the tools it needs to correct imbalances and right itself. Giving up the foods that have been keeping you sick is nothing to be sad about. Instead rejoice! The truth about food will set you free. I believe that every choice we make is like a drop of water in an ocean. While small, that drop of water can send ripples around the world.

This information is not meant to make you crazy or to make you feel bad about yourself for not being perfect. True perfection is recognizing we are part of a whole, complete even with flaws. We can not make a mistake. We can only experience and move on. And yes, sometimes I break my own rules. I would rather you cheat healthy with the cooked fruit and poor food combining in the Very Berry Coffee Cake on pages 36 and 37 than with a commercial store bought coffee cake. That is why I feel this is an excellent transitional guide for taking you to the next level. These recipes will give you healthy, safer, comfort foods for those times when you just can't eat one more salad.

I want to believe that common sense is still alive and well. If it is not naturally found in nature

Don't: ▶ Breath it   ▶ Watch it   ▶ Drink It   ▶ Listen to it
          ▶ Eat It   ▶ Put it on your skin ▶ Inject it in your body **Period!**

There are so many wonderful natural products out there today for us to use that are earth and animal friendly that we have no excuse other than habit or ignorance to do other wise. Self-help books are everywhere. Natural food markets are becoming common place and the internet now puts the world at our finger tips. When our shopping carts aren't filled with cookies, ice cream, low fat granola bars, coffee, artificial coffee creamers, soda, wheat products, cheese, lunch meat, potato chips, frozen dinners and candy, it leaves quite a bit of extra cash in the budget for fresh whole organic fruits and vegetables.

In Yoga we are taught that deep cleansing breaths are healing. Some Yogi masters believe that we are each born with our own set amount of breaths. The faster and more shallow we breath, the shorter time we have to experience life. So it is to our benefit to take long, slow, deep breaths because in doing so we can double the amount of time we have on this planet. When we quiet our mind, it has no choice but to listen to our heart. Free of toxic thoughts, we can ask simple uncluttered questions, becoming a conduit for universal truths; **Who am I? What is my purpose? How do I fit in with the plan?** For me, food is the gateway for connecting higher intelligence to earth energy. Without air, water or food, this experience we call life would be very short lived indeed. Without clean air, clean water and clean food, yes we continue to exist, but do we truly live as intended?

I focus on food because it is my medium. But it isn't only about natural organic foods and pure water. It's also about other invasions into our immune systems. Please consider the research done by such people as Horowitz, Emoto, Young, Trudeau and Myss. Read what they have to say about important health-related issues. It is your Constitutional right to be able to make decisions about your own health. Everyone else is a consultant. Read and listen to both sides of an issue before taking action. Always make informed decisions regarding your health and wellness. You and you alone will live and die with the consequences. Read books that talk about basic fundamental core issues. Find out what Leonard Horowitz has to say about vaccinations in his book, "Emerging Viruses," or Masaro Emoto on water in "The Hidden Messages in Water," Robert O. Young on the topic of pH in "Sick & Tired?" or "The pH Miracle," Kevin Trudeau's "Natural Cures They Don't Want You to Know About" and "Anatomy of the Spirit" by Caroline Myss.

As soon as an author tells me to follow this exact plan, take my product and it will fix you, I get a little nervous. One or two products, no matter how good, will not fix anything if we continue to perpetuate bad habits. There are many paths to the mountain top. I like to think that once at the top all of our paths have lead us to the truth. Universal truth has no judgement, regret, denial, fancy packaging or slogans. When we are taking seven different medications, sleeping on polyester bedding scented with dryer sheets, living on caffeine and sugar, drinking tap water, eating and drinking dairy products, watching five plus hours of television a day, are being bombarded with electromagnetic waves without protection and have not walked barefoot on chemical-free grass in years (or perhaps ever); how can we be expected to regain even the basics for wellness? This isn't about some "program for wellness," this is about "THE program for wellness," and I am not the one who put it together!

In our modern society, people are more concerned about the chemicals they put into their swimming pool than the chemicals they put into the living body of water contained inside of them, the human blood. Every cell is a dynamic living organism. Every cell matters. High vibration foods make us well (anabolic) and too many low vibration foods make us sick (catabolic). I encourage you to eat low on the food chain and high on the vibrational frequency. I continue practicing my mission statement of: Healing people, one bite of food at a time.

Thank you for purchasing this book. It shows you are flexible and open to new ideas about old concepts. Be sure to visit our website: www.feelgoodfood.com where you will find more information and products to help heal a small planet, one person at a time.

In the Spirit of Peace, and the Fullness of Love.

Introduction

If you or a loved one have been avoiding allergenic foods or your body pH has been out of balance for a while, I hope I can add a little variety to your diet. If this is new to you, welcome. There are many wonderful books and cookbooks on the market filled with ideas, recipes and helpful hints. My goal is to put the information you will need to be successful in this new way of eating in one place, at your fingertips.

Being different isn't easy. It doesn't take very long to realize that avoiding foods common to the standard American diet makes us different. The situation becomes more difficult as more allergenic foods, pollens, chemicals and additives are uncovered. If you are allergic to one or two things, making the adjustments necessary will require a few planning strategies, but on the whole should not be difficult. However, if all of the foods you have grown up with are the cause of your chronic illness, major changes must be made in order to become well. Feeling good, looking fit and enjoying life to its fullest is your right. Don't allow advertising hype and peer pressure to keep you from it.

Every time we turn on the TV or radio, we are being told by people who know nothing about us, or our individual needs, what will make us better. It's everywhere — papers, magazines even unwanted free samples in the mail. Protecting our children from it is an almost overwhelming task, from hot lunch programs at school to meeting friends at a favorite fast food hangout.

Then there are the social implications. Let's face it, we live in a time where everyone has a "food, folks and fun" mentality. Unfortunately, the price we pay for this quick and easy lifestyle is our health and happiness and the health and happiness of all future generations. In my opinion, that is a steep price to pay for something we have been told we need by strangers, whose only motivation is profit. Listen to your body. You are the only person who knows what you need.

Every member of my family has food allergies along with various other sensitivities. My first introduction to food allergies was when my youngest son, Zach, was born. Looking back, he was having allergic reactions even before he was born. By the time Zach was two, my husband and I knew something was wrong. Once we got over the "whose side of the family did this come from game," we realized the apple never falls far from the tree. In time, we were all on the program and problems of a lifetime began to vanish.

First and foremost, become a label reader. Find out what is in everything you and yours eat, drink, breathe, wear and come in contact with. If you have not done so yet you are in for quite a shock. When we first found out Zach was to avoid wheat, dairy, eggs, soy, corn,

Zach starts college this year. Wow!

chocolate, food coloring, preservatives and sugar, I was numb. It didn't get better. After three hours at the supermarket I had shopped in since childhood, I was horrified when I discovered those ingredients were in everything! I was only able to purchase a couple of things, and the novelty of dry rice cakes doesn't last long. Feeling sorry for yourself and crying doesn't go very far either.

If we were going to help Zach I had to learn a new way. Soon I knew my way around the local health food store, joined an organic food co-op, joined an organic produce co-op and started baking everyday. I started eating with my son on his rotation, eliminating the same foods he did. It seemed cruel to eat a family dinner and serve my little boy something different and less appetizing. To my amazement, I lost weight and started to feel great. I had always considered myself a good cook. Why should changing ingredients change that?

Allergies have grown to almost epidemic proportions due to pollutants and convenience foods. I was fortunate. I had the support of family and friends and the luxury to be able to stay home and do what I had to do. But what about people who weren't as fortunate as I? It is not my nature to suffer in silence and before long people I had never met were calling me for recipes and advice. I knew there were people who did not have the loving support of a husband or worked full time and couldn't do all the research and baking. There were also people who lived in rural areas and did not have access to all of the wonderful sources I did living in a suburb of Chicago.

I have gathered so much information over the past 15 years that sorting it out has been my biggest challenge. This cookbook is geared to the diversified rotary diet my family has been following. If you have already established a rotation that works for you, I hope the format of my recipes will make the necessary substitutions easy. If you are allergic to two members of a food family, chances are all members of that family are suspect and should be avoided or at the very least rotated. As far as the rotation, I have found that four days is not enough for some foods. These foods can be tolerated at eight or even twelve day intervals, some not at all.

In the beginning it will be important to eat simply and keep a log. If you always eat the same foods together, separate them until you are sure of the true culprit. Examples would be

Introduction

tomatoes and basil or garlic and onions or wheat and sugar. To help clear up any confusion, I am also including a list of food families, pages 10 thru 17. Did you know Canola oil comes from the rapeseed, a relative to the mustard plant? So if you are allergic to mustard it would not be a good idea to use Canola oil every day.

Consider this book a guide. Fuel your body with as much care as you fuel your automobile. I don't think anyone would put diesel fuel into a car that only takes regular octane. Eat to live, don't live to eat. Eating as close to nature as possible will bring us to a natural state of wellness. I am not asking anyone to drop to their knees and graze. What I am suggesting is to eliminate over-processed foods, hormones, pesticides, dyes and preservatives.

Allergies to foods are the by-product of a weakened immune system. Look around your home and community. Are there pollutants compromising your immune balance? Are you sensitive to the polyester in your clothes? The formaldehyde in your carpeting, the plastic your lunches are wrapped in? Manufacturers use chemicals to bind fragrances to their products. By themselves these factors probably are harmless, however, the sum of the whole can be devastating.

Look to other cultures and cuisines, check out my reading suggestions. Foods that tasted "bad" while eating an unhealthy diet everyday may taste delightful with your cleansed taste buds. Good luck. Always remember you are not alone. Being well should not be a struggle, but rather a natural state of well being.

The following information is not meant to replace the advice of a qualified health care professional. Likewise do not discontinue any prescription medication without consulting a medical doctor. However, you may find that in time, medication may need to be adjusted and frequent doctor visits unnecessary. How can changing the foods you eat reduce the amount of medication you ask? Give this new way of thinking, eating and living one month and the answer may present itself. As my mother always said, "the proof is in the pudding"!

Chronic sinus and ear infections may disappear when you eliminate all dairy from your diet. Arthritis symptoms may lessen or even disappear when all nightshade vegetables (potatoes, tomatoes, peppers, eggplant and tobacco) and pork (all forms) are eliminated. Perhaps by cutting out wheat, the extra weight that has been stubbornly hanging on for years will suddenly melt away.

My personal food hit list to avoid includes. but is not limited to: ALL forms of pork, ALL crustacean, ALL fish without scales, ALL dairy, ALL tap water, ALL forms of refined sugar and flour, ALL foods containing hydrogenated oils, MSG and last but not least ALL processed foods and chemical additives that may be added along the way.

I make no claim to be a great medical genius, quite the contrary. All I have to offer is a love of good food and a creative way of preparing it. I offer no miracle cure other than the miracle of the human body to heal itself when given a chance. I offer many self-help books on my web site www.feelgoodfood.com. Please find the time and read some of these books with an open mind and heart.

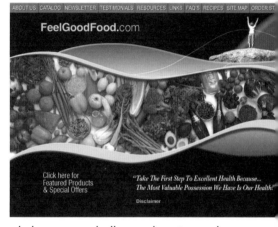

You may wish to investigate other alternative healing methods. The practice of meditation and Yoga leads to a balancing of mind and body, allowing us to find contentment and avoid "dis-ease." Foot Reflexology sends powerful healing messages to every organ and cell of your body via nerve endings in your feet. Massage soothes jangled nerves and allows relaxation and a break from stress. Aroma therapy, homeopathy, kinesiology, acupuncture, cranial-sacral therapy or chiropractic are only a few of the options.

Exercise is a must. It will allow the toxins to leave your body more quickly. A 30 minute walk every day is enough or a gentle rebounder workout is the perfect whole body aerobic exercise for those cold or rainy days. Speaking of overcast days, find some full spectrum lights and put them in your home.

The proper vitamin, mineral and herb therapy along with pH balance will also help. More guidance than I have to offer will be needed. Seek out the programs and the people who can help you find what's right for you. A simple hair analysis will tell of your particular deficiencies and toxic metal levels.

Candida and food sensitivities usually go hand in hand. In addition to avoiding the foods that give you trouble, you will also need to avoid ALL sugars including fruit juice, natural sugars, refined sugar and no more than one piece of unbruised fresh fruit a day; ALL ferments

Introduction

including alcohol, soy sauce and vinegar; ALL molds including aged cheeses, tempe, miso, dried fruit, cold cereals and raw nuts; ALL fungi including mushrooms and yeast, until the situation is under control. If any of this information is new to you, your poor little brain is now on circuit overload! One way to simplify the problem is to become an avid label reader. But what does all that stuff on the label mean? A good rule of thumb is if you can't pronounce it or you don't know what it means, don't put it in your trusting body or the body of anyone you love. Wait a minute you say, the FDA has approved all of these additives and preservative. Perhaps alone each ingredient is safe. However, the harm comes when you add them all together along with pollution in both water and air, chemicals in the treated water, chemicals used in agriculture, chemicals and antibiotics fed livestock (including chicken and fish), chemical fragrances, etc. Then multiply that by the number meals you have consumed and the number of breaths you breath and the years you have lived.

We live in a time when just about everyone is zinc deficient. Zinc used to be found in abundance in vegetables and grain. But over time, because of modern farming practices and the use of chemical fertilizers, the soil has been leached of zinc. Now we are not even getting the small amount we need without using supplements.

Common sense tells me something is wrong when natural nutrients are removed from processed foods and then chemically added back in. I will pass along to you the same advice that was given to me: don't take my word for it - read - read- read!

Follow the 80-20 rule: 80% alkalizing organic raw vegetables and non-sweet fruit and 20% healthy acid-forming foods. Many of the recipes in this book are considered transitional or part of the 20%. It is up to you to get the 80% raw vegetables in your body every day!

As long as you are alive it is never too late to feel healthy. Instead of feeling sorry for yourself, be grateful to have found something you can do before it's too late! Life is a glorious adventure. I have personally seen miracles brought about by a change in diet. ■

Food Basics

Helpful Tips

For most of us, how we feel about the food we eat has been ingrained since birth. Some people may need to go cold turkey in order for a change to work. Others, however, need a slower, more transitional way of dealing with food. I was among the latter group. Perhaps in the beginning just cutting out the dairy will be radical enough. That in itself should make you feel a great deal better. Next, try cutting out refined sugars and chemical additives. Next wheat and corn. If you can cut out one harmful food a month ,just think of the difference it will make in one year. Attitude will do wonders. Instead of looking at the food you have given up and feeling deprived, consider yourself a natural foods gourmet. In reality, all you have given up are some bad habits and ill health. What you will gain is a second chance to enjoy life and feel wonderful!

Your taste buds will adjust. . . and so will your body.

The following is a list of helpful hints and tips followed by other information you may find useful.

▶ Bake don't fry. If you do fry, never allow the oil to smoke. The smoke means the oil has become too hot and is being converted from polyunsaturated (healthy) to saturated (unhealthy) fat. Organic coconut oil is excellent for frying and baking because of its high smoke temperature. If you need to add oil to a recipe, add once cooking is completed. Use just enough oil to season a pan and keep things from sticking. Many of my recipes say to bake before frying to dry out the outer crust so the food won't become a sponge for the oil.

▶ Please, oh please, use only expeller pressed or cold pressed oils. If the oil does not say expeller or cold pressed, chemicals and/or heat have been used to extract the oil. Never, never use anything that has been hydrogenated.

▶ If you go to a hardware store, you can buy 1" bristle brushes for far less than a pastry brush. Keep one for each oil you use (write the type of oil on the handle) and use to brush pans and baking surfaces. Some specialty stores also have spray bottles made for oil and will not clog.

▶ You are now asking yourself, I have gone from one brand of oil to eight, how do I keep it all straight? There are two schools of thought. I have a friend who keeps one shelf in her pantry for each day of the rotation, labeled day one, day two, etc. The second method is the one I use, a plastic lazy susan, the kind you find in the grocery or department store. The 11" size works great. A quick spin places the oil you need at your fingertips. For more ideas, see tools page 26.

▶ Read ALL labels, nothing is as it seems. If you can't pronounce it or you aren't sure of the source, don't use it! Be suspicious of anything in a can or cellophane wrapper. Remember there are thousands of ingredients used in food processing that, under law, do not need to be shown on the label! Beware of the word natural — it usually means MSG, corn, soy or some other chemically produced mystery ingredient. Last but not least, not everything in the health food store is healthy. Read labels there, too.

▶ Candida and sugar. More than likely, if you have food allergies or an acid pH, Candida albicans plays a role and may be the cause of the sensitivities. Anything sweet is sugar: dextrose, fructose, rice syrup, barley malt syrup, maple sugar and syrup, sucanat, agave nectar, xylitol, molasses, turbinado, fruit juice that has been squeezed more than a few minutes, honey, etc. Even fresh fruit contains sugars and should be eaten sparingly on an empty stomach with nothing to follow for a half hour. See my notes at the bottom of the recipe pages. The only exception is stevia.

▶ Refined grains also will convert quickly to sugar, as will alcohol and milk. In my opinion, sugar is the hardest thing to give up. It is the most carcinogenic ingredient in cigarettes and a factor that makes them so addictive. Sugar is the first thing we give a baby after mother's milk. Chemically speaking, there is only one molecule difference between sugarcane and cocaine.

▶ The only sweet that is safe to use, other than fresh fruit in moderation, is the herb stevia. Stevia has been used in the Orient and Europe for years and has just recently been approved by our government for internal use here. Studies have shown stevia is good for the pancreas and may be able to help regulate blood sugar and blood pressure. Another good choice is low-glycemic Agave Nectar (made from a cactus) in place of honey. Xylitol is another good choice since it is low-glycemic and non-fermentable. If you can not find these items in your local store, try us on-line: www.feelgoodfood.com.

▶ For shopping, organic food cooperatives are found just about everywhere. Look for one in your area. Their convenience and prices can not be beat, Grow fresh herbs in pots on window-sills. When weather permits, grow a victory garden. Become friends with the owner/manager of the local health food store. I have found them to be a wealth of knowledge and good for moral support. Health food supermarkets also are beginning to appear around the country. Even your local supermarket may carry some organic fruits and vegetables and, if they do not, talk to the manager. For other options go to pages 186-188.

▶ Organic and minimally processed. I can not stress enough the importance of organic and minimally processed foods. Remove yourself from as many chemicals as possible. Mother knows best. If it is not a naturally occurring substance found in nature, be wary. You may want to consult with a healthcare professional to determine if some additional measures need to be taken to rid your body of unwanted toxins.

▶ Use sea salt in place of table salt. Because sea salt is saltier, you will need less. It also contains a larger concentration of healthful minerals. If salt is iodized, it also has added sugar, necessary to keep the iodine from clumping the salt. If you are concerned about sufficient iodine, eat kelp. Switch to Real Salt™ brand or a good sea salt and avoid processed or ionized salt. I use Dr. Bronner's Balanced Mineral Salt™ and Vegetable Bouillon. Spike is also good. There are several others. Read the labels for your needs. One of the best commercial salts in the world comes from Hawaii, it's red and called Alae. See if you can find some.

▶ Our bodies make protein from amino acids, not protein. Protein foods are broken down into amino acids. As Americans eating our SAD (Standard American Diet), diets as much as 30 to 40% of our caloric intake is protein. For some people, too much protein and not enough fresh vegetables could contribute to an increased acid condition, which could lead to poor calcium absorption (refer to the Food Combining Chart on page 25). So all of that milk and cheese you have been eating and drinking for strong bones and teeth may have been leading towards osteoporosis not to mention arthritis, sinus infections and cardiovascular disease. To order a simple Home Test pH Test Kit, go to www.feelgoodfood.com.

▶ The myth that all four food groups need to be represented on your plate at every meal is just that - a myth. In fact, eating them together could cause indigestion at the very least. As long as all of the food groups are eaten within a four-day span, you are fine.

▶ Water from a pure source should become your beverage of choice. A distiller for your home is a great idea. If you are drinking distilled water, be sure to add a squeeze of fresh lemon juice or a few grains of sea salt or good trace mineral. However, do not drink anything with a meal or within 20 minutes before or after. It dilutes the stomach acids sent to digest the food and will slow down the whole digestive process. Drink at least half your body weight in ounces of good water from a pure source every day away from meals.

▶ Be cautious of dry teas and herbs that may harbor mold. To help keep the candida in check, try some Pau d'Arco tea, also known as La Pasho or Taheebo. This tea comes from the bark of a tree in the Amazon Rainforest. The wood from this tree has a fire rating of A1 (the same as concrete), is denser than water (it sinks) and is insect resistant.

▶ Never, never, never use a microwave oven to thaw, warm-up or cook your food. It changes the energetic structure of the food. On an energetic level, your body will now only recognize a portion of the food factors from the receptor side of the cells.

▶ Stay away from any product that has a fragrance added to it. Fragrance is nothing more than a chemical added to hide the smell of other chemicals. Use a laundry ball to wash your clothes, and dryer balls in place of fabric softener, invest in a good air purifier for your home. ■

Four Day Rotation

Why rotate food? Good question. We spend a lifetime under the delusion that we are eating a healthy diet. Remember the four basic food groups from grammar school and actually being paranoid about getting sufficient servings of each one at every meal? The food pyramid now being used still leaves out a great deal of information. The correct size of a single serving is not made clear. No mention is ever made of food combining or good fat verses bad fat or the importance of diversity and organic and minimally processed.

Day 1

Day 2

In the beginning, keep a chart of everything you eat — everything — and how you feel as the day progresses. By rotating your food, a clear picture of what you are sensitive to will begin to emerge. Also eat simply to unmask the culprit. Keep eliminating suspect foods until you have a diet that makes you feel good. This may take a month or two, but if you are persistent a definite pattern will emerge. Another reason to rotate foods is to allow your body to recover (it takes about three days) from a hidden allergen. You may even wish to figure out an eight-day rotation. Perhaps a seven-day menu you don't even have to think about after you have figured it out once. For example, every Monday eat a spinach and lettuce Breakfast Salad with sunflower seeds and artichoke hearts (page 48-49) Raspberry Dressing (page 97) for breakfast and a second salad for lunch with Quinoa Crackers (pages 66-67) on the side. A handful of pistachios for an afternoon snack. Whole Quinoa Pilaf (pages 116-117) for dinner with a side of beets or greens. Have a snack of sunflower seeds around 8:00 if still hungry. Nothing in that menu is any harder to fix or obtain than what you have been using — just different. After a while it will become second nature.

Think about it, Americans eat the same six or so foods every day, day in and day out. Wheat, yeast, eggs, sugar, corn in some form, soy, dairy and beef. When you think of nature's abundance, how can this be variety? However, when you first cut these things out, you will feel there is nothing else to eat! You will discover the true meaning of variety and find eating at a different fast food place every day for lunch was rearranging the same six foods. What we should be eating is vegetables, whole grains and more vegetables. Did I mention you should be eating tons of fresh seasonal vegetables!

Day 3

Day 4

If you already suspect certain foods are causing problems, cut them out of your first rotation and add the suspect foods back in one at a time, so a true evaluation can be made. Another suggestion is to make several copies of the chart on pages 6 and 7 and personalize it by crossing out the foods you are avoiding. Carry one copy with you and keep a second taped to the inside of a kitchen cabinet for easy reference. A different color marker can be used for each family member and a simple key made. Good luck, I know you can do it.

Some of the foods in the following chart are meant for information purposes only. I feel, for example, that pork, shrimp and dairy should not be eaten under any circumstances. Also tomatoes, potatoes, peppers, eggplant and tobacco should not be eaten (or smoked) because of the potential inflammatory problems they can cause to bones and joints. However, that decision is not mine to make. ■

Days One & Two of Rotation

Highlighted foods indicate a change in food families only - highlights DO NOT indicate a "better" food choice.

	DAY ONE	DAY TWO
FRUIT FRESH & DRIED	Mulberry, Fig, Breadfruit, **Kiwi**, Strawberry, Raspberry, Blackberry, Boysenberry, Rose Hips, **Grapes**, Mango	Plum, Cherry, Peach, Apricot, Nectarine, Wild Cherry, **Pineapple**, Guava, **Papaya**, **Papain**, Paw Paw
DRINK	Tomato Juice, **Grape Juice**, Rose Hip Tea, **Chamomile Tea**, Goat & Cow Milk, **Coffee**, (any Juice or Tea from any day one item)	Cherry Juice, Prune Juice, Peach Juice, Apricot Juice, **Pineapple Juice**, Papaya Juice, **Carrot Juice**, Barley Coffee, **(any Juice or Tea from any day two item)**
SWEET & SOUR	Beet Sugar, **Maple Sugar**, **Maple Syrup**, Raisins, Wine Vinegar, **Yogurt**, **Buttermilk**, Cream of Tartar, **Pickled Ginger**	Clover Honey, **Raw Unprocessed Cane Sugar**, **Sorghum Molasses**, Brown Rice Syrup, Brown Rice Vinegar, Barley Syrup, **Umeboshi Plum**, **Ume Plum Vinegar**
SEEDS NUTS & OILS	Cashew, Pistachio, **Macadamia**, Sunflower Seed, Sunflower Oil, Safflower Oil, **Flax Seed**, Flax Oil, Butter, Ghee, **Grapeseed Oil**	Almond, Almond Oil, Apricot Kernel, **Sesame Seed**, **Tahini or Oil**, Chestnut, Brazil, **Soy Nut**, **Soy Bean Oil**, **Miso**, **Tamari**, **Soy Butter**, **Soy Sauce**, Corn Oil
FISH	Salt Water Fish, Abalone Squid, Clam, Mussel, Oyster, Scallop, **Halibut**, **Haddock**, **Red Snapper**, **Shark**, Anchovy, **Cod**	Fresh Water Fish, **Crab**, **Crayfish**, **Lobster**, **Prawn**, **Shrimp**, Smelt, Pike
MEAT	**Lamb**, **Goat**, **Llama**, Beef, Beef Liver, Veal, Veal Liver, Gelatin, All Dairy (both **Goat** and Cow)	Chicken, Cornish Hen, Pheasant, Quail, (plus their livers and eggs), **Venison**, **Venison Liver**, Ostrich
SEA VEGGIES	Dulse	Wakame, Agar-Agar, Nori, Hijiki, Arame
VEGGIES	Potato, Tomato, Eggplant, Pepper, Pimento, (Tobacco), **Beet**, **Spinach**, **Swiss Chard**, Romaine, Sunchoke, Chicory, Lettuce, Endive, Escarole, Dandelion, Artichoke	Mushroom, Yeast, **Carrot**, **Parsnip**, **Celery**, **Parsley**, Water Chestnuts, **Sweet Potato**, Soybean, Lecithin, Miso Tofu, **Jicama**
GRAINS & STARCHES	Potato Flour, **Tapioca Flour**, Quinoa, **Yucca**	(Grass Family), Wheat, Corn, Rice, Oat, Barley, Millet, Rye, Bamboo Shoots, Wild Rice, **Jicama Starch**
SPICES	Nutmeg, Mace, **Chili Pepper**, **Paprika**, **Cayenne**, **Curry**, Tarragon, Ginger, **Turmeric**, **Cardamom**	Anise, Dill, Fennel, Cumin, Parsley, Coriander, Caraway, **Allspice**, **Clove**, **Vanilla**, Asafetida

Days Three & Four of Rotation

Always keep a family together, see Food Families pages 10 thru 17 – Never eat the same food every day

	DAY THREE	DAY FOUR
FRUIT FRESH & DRIED	Apple, (Pectin), Pear, Quince, **Melon, Watermelon, Cantaloupe, etc.,** Blueberry, Cranberry, Huckleberry, Currant, Gooseberry, **Persimmon**	Banana, Plantain, **Lemon, Orange, Tangelo, Grapefruit, Lime, Tangerine, Kumquat, Ugli Fruit,** Pomegranate, **Date,** Carob, **Olive**
DRINK	Apple Juice and Cider, **Cranberry Juice (unsweetened),** Wintergreen Tea, Green and Black Tea, **Pau d' Arco Tea,** (any Juice or Tea from any day three item)	Orange Juice, Lemonade, Grapefruit Juice, **Lemon Balm Tea,** Mint Tea, **Carob Tea,** (any Juice or Tea from any day four item)
SWEET & SOUR	**Stevia,** Apple or Pear Juice Concentrate, Apple Cider Vinegar, **Sauerkraut Juice,** Agave Nectar	Date Sugar, **Tupelo or Orange Blossom or Alfalfa Honey or any** source other than Clover
SEEDS NUTS & OILS	Filbert/Hazel Nut, Xylitol made from Birch, **Poppy Seed,** Pumpkin and Squash Seed, **Cotton Seed Oil,** Canola Oil, **Lard,** Palm Kernel Oil	Walnut, Walnut Oil, Pecan, **Pine Nut,** Coconut, Coconut Oil, **Peanut** and **Peanut Oil,** Olive Oil
FISH	Salt Water Fish, Scrod, Ocean Perch, Turbot, Orange Roughy, Flounder, Monk Fish, Sole, Tuna, Mahi Mahi	Fresh Water Fish, Whitefish, Salmon, Herring, Catfish, Lake Trout, Lake Perch, Bass
MEAT	Pork, (Ham, Bacon, Liver, Lard), **Game other than from another day,** Buffalo	Duck, Turkey, Goose, (plus their livers and eggs), **Rabbit**
SEA VEGGIES	Kelp, Spirulina, Bluegreen Algae	Kombu
VEGGIES	Cucumber, Pumpkin, All Squash, Zucchini, **Turnip, Kale, Radish, Mustard Greens, Cabbage, Broccoli, Brussels Sprout, Rutabaga, Cauliflower, Horseradish, Bok Choy,** Watercress, **Okra,** Sorrel, **Rhubarb**	All Dried Beans, Pea, Lentil, Chick Pea, Green Bean, Alfalfa Snow Pea, Bean Threads, **Onion, Garlic, Asparagus, Chives, Leeks, Aloe, Shallots,** Avocado
GRAINS & STARCHES	Buckwheat, Amaranth, **Arrowroot, Starch**	Chick Pea Flour, **Spelt, Kamut, Teff,** Dasheen, Nami, Poi, Taro, **Kudzu (or Kuzu)**
SPICES	Mustard Seed, Horseradish, **Poppy Seed,** Pepper (Black and White), **Oil of Birch (Wintergreen)**	**Citron,** Mint, Spearmint, Peppermint, Basil, Sage, Thyme, Oregano, Horehound, Savory, Marjoram, Rosemary, **Garlic, Onion, Chive,** Licorice, **Cinnamon,** Bay Leaf, **Cocoa**

Food Families

PLANT KINGDOM: It is important to be aware of the relatives to the foods to which you are allergic. An example would be the nightshade family. If you are sensitive to tomatoes and peppers, look closely at potatoes, eggplant and tobacco. Karaya gum, a close relative to the cola nut, is used as the base for India Ink. Many newspapers, typewriter ribbons and computer printouts use this type of ink. I have never been able to read a newspaper. My vision would blur, nose run, eyes itch and my brain would become foggy. I am allergic to cola. Half a beer and I am falling down drunk; I was allergic to barley, hops, and had a candida overgrowth. Never assume food is pure. For example buckwheat hulls are often mixed with commercial black pepper as filler. Corn oil is sprayed on the interior of most canned goods and be aware of exactly what the "natural coloring" is in what you are eating. One example is paprika, which is fine unless you have a problem with the nightshade family.

Avoiding all processed foods, eating fresh organic foods and being an informed consumer is the safest way to be and stay healthy. It would be impossible to share everything I have learned. Don't rely on me. Read and research for yourself and don't despair. Remember, nature never intended for us to eat processed foods. How can anyone improve on nature and the natural order of the universe?

PLANT (PLANTAE) KINGDOM

ALLIUM (ALLIACEAE) FAMILY: Chinese Lotus, Chives, Garlic, Iris, Leek, Lily, Onion, Shallots, Welsh Onion, Yucca

ARUM (ARACEAE) FAMILY: Dasheen, Malanga, Poi, Taro, Yautia

ASPARAGUS (ASPARAGACEAE) FAMILY: Asparagus (was formerly placed in the Lily Family)

ASTER (COMPOSITAE) FAMILY: Artichoke (common), Burdock, Calendula, Chamomile, Chicory, Chrysanthemum, Daisy, Dandelion, Endive, Escarole, Goldenrod, Jerusalem Artichoke (the tuber of the Sunflower plant), Lettuce All Types, Marigold, Oyster Plant, Ragweed, Safflower, Sagebrush, Stevia, Sunflower (possible source of levulose and fructose), Tarragon, Thistle, Wormwood, Yarrow, Zinnia

AMARANTH (AMARANTHACEAE) FAMILY: Amaranth, Beet, Goosefoot, Pigweed, Quinoa, Spinach, Swiss Chard

ARROWROOT (MARANTACEAE) FAMILY: Arrowroot, Prayer Plant

BANANA (MUSACEAE) FAMILY: Common Banana (technically the berry of an herb bush), Dwarf Banana, Gros Michel, Plantain

Note: I do not recommend eating or using some of the foods, plants and animals listed. They are here for informational purposes only. ALSO, please note: Foods are listed by family not genus within the family.

BEECH (FAGACEAE) FAMILY: Beechnut American, European and Spanish - Chestnut American, Chinese and Spanish

BIRCH (BETULACEAE) FAMILY: Filbert, Hazelnut (same nut at different stages of maturity), Xylitol

BUCKWHEAT (POLYGONACEAE) FAMILY: Buckwheat, Garden Sorrel, Joint Weed, Knot Weed, Rhubarb, Sea Grape, Smart Weed, Sorrel, Umbrella Plant

CANNABIS (CANNABACEAE) FAMILY: Bhang, Dagga, Ganja, Hashish, Hemp, Hops, Jute, Marijuana

CHICLE (SAPODILLA) FAMILY: Chicle (Gum from the latex of the Sapodilla used as the chief ingredient of chewing gum), Naseberry, Sapodilla Fruit

CITRUS (RUTACEAE) FAMILY: Angostura (bitters), Blood Orange, Citrange, Citron, Common Orange , Grapefruit, Kumquat, Lemon, Lime, Mandarin Orange, Navel Orange, Sour Orange, Tangerine, Ugli Fruit

COCOA (STERCULIA) FAMILY: Chocolate, Cocoa, Cola, India Ink, Sterculia Gum, Tragacanth Gum

EBONY (EBENACEAE) FAMILY: Persimmon

EVENING PRIMROSE (ONAGRACEAE) FAMILY: Evening Primrose Oil, Suncups, Sundrops

FLAX (LINACEAE) FAMILY: Flax Seed, Flax Oil, Linen, Linseed Oil (ink & varnish)

*FUNGI FAMILY: Bacterial Cultures (Yogurt, Kefir, Aged Cheeses, Miso, Sourdough, Tempe, Soy Sauce), Common Wild Mushroom, Commercial Mushroom, Mold (on Melons, Dried Fruit, Tea, Leftovers), Yeast (Alcoholic Beverages, Vinegar, Most B-Vitamins), etc.

GINGER (ZINGIBERACEAE) FAMILY: Blue Ginger, Cardamom, Curry, Ginger, Myoga, Thi Ginger, Turmeric (Oleoresin "natural" coloring in food or "beta carotene"),

GINSENG (ARALIACEAE) FAMILY: American Ginseng, American Spikenard, Panax Ginseng, (Siberian Ginseng is a distant relative), Sarsaparilla (used with Birch Oil to make Root Beer)

*GLUTEN-FREE (MANY FOOD FAMILIES): Amaranth, Arrowroot, Buckwheat, Carob Flour, Corn, Garbanzo Flour, Flour made from Beans, Legumes, Nuts, Millet, Potato Flour, Quinoa, Poi, Rice, Sago, Soy, Soy Flour, Tapioca, Teff, Xanthan Gum. NOTE: Always check for possible cross contamination.

*GLUTEN GRAINS (GRAMINEAE FAMILY): The following list is for the grain and substances made from the grain only, there is NO gluten in the grasses sprouted from these grains; Barley, Barley Malt, Kamut, Oat, Rye (Pumpernickel), Semolina, Spelt, Triticale, Wheat, Wheat Bran, Vinegar made from grain, White Flour. NOTE: Commercial Breading, Cookies, Corn Bread, Rye Bread, Soy Sauce, Thickened Sauces, White Bread, etc. Read all labels, call the manufacturer if you are not sure.

GOURD (CUCURBITACEAE) FAMILY: Cucumber, Pickles, Indian Gherkin, (All Melons) Cantaloupe, Casaba, Honeydew, Muskmelon, Watermelon, etc., Pumpkin, (All Squash) Winter, Acorn, Summer, Zucchini, etc.

*Note: Not an "official" food family, listed for informational purposed only.

Food Families

GRAPE (VITACEAE) FAMILY: Brandy, Champagne, Cream of Tartar, Grape all varieties, Raisin all varieties, Baking Powder (Tartaric Acid), Muscadine Grape, Slip-Skin Grape, Wine made from Grape, Wine Vinegar

GRASS (GRAMINEAE) FAMILY: Bamboo, Bamboo Shoots, Barley (Beer), Barley Malt, Browntop, Corn (Cellulose, Dextrose, Glucose), Kamut, Millet, Oats, Spelt, Sugar Cane (Sucrose, Turbinado, Rum, Sucanat, Sugar, Molasses, Kafir, Sorghum), Wheat (Bran, Durum, Germ, Gluten, Graham, Semolina, Triticale), Wild Oats, Rice (all), Rye (Pumpernickel), Teff NOTE: Kamut, Spelt, Teff are distant relatives to modern wheat, these non-hybrid varieties may be tolerated by some wheat sensitive people.

HEATH (ERICACEAE) FAMILY: Azaleas, Blueberry, Checkerberry, Cranberry, Currant, Gooseberry, Heaths, Heather, Huckleberry, Rhododendron, Wintergreen

KIWIFRUIT (ACTINIDIACEAE) FAMILY: Chinese Gooseberry, Kiwi (fruit is considered a large berry)

LAUREL (LAURACEAE) FAMILY: Alligator Pear, Avocado, Avocado Pear, Bay leaf, Camphor, Cinnamon, Gumbo File, Sassafras

LEGUME (FABACEAE) FAMILY: Acacia, Acacia Gum, Alfalfa, Beans all varieties; Aduki, Black, Black-eye Pea, Bush, Kidney, Lentil, Navy, etc., Carob, Cassia (also called Senna, used in Cinnamon and Curry), Chick Pea (Garbanzo), Clover, Cowpea, Fenugreek (primary ingredient in imitation Maple Syrup), Gar Gum, Green Bean, Gum Acacia, Gum Arabic, Jicama, Licorice, Lima Bean, Locust Bean Gum, Soybean, Mexican Turnip, Mung Bean (Bean Threads, Bean Sprouts), Pea, Peanut, Peanut Oil, Pigeon Pea, Snow Pea, Spanish Pea, String Bean, Tamarind, Tofu, Tragacanth Gum, Yam Bean, Urd Flour, Xanthan gum (sometimes produced from the fermentation of corn sugar, know your source)

MADDER (RUBIACEAE) FAMILY: Alizarin (natural red dye), Coffee Bean, Ipecac, Quinine (bark)

MALLOW (MALVACEAE) FAMILY: Cotton, Cotton Seed Oil, Hibiscus (Red Zinger Tea), Okra

MAPLE (ACERACEAE) FAMILY: Maple Syrup, Maple Sugar

MINT (LAMIACEAE) FAMILY: Balm, Basil (used in perfumes, tulsi and herb scented room fresheners), Bergamot, Betony, Catnip, Chia, Clary, Dropsy Plant, Horehound, Hyssop, Lavender, Lemon Balm, Marjoram, Melissa, Menthol, Mint, Oregano, Pennyroyal, Peppermint, Rosemary, Sage, St. Joseph Wart, Savory, Spearmint, Summer Savory, Sweet Balm, Thyme

MORNING GLORY (CONVOLVULACEAE) FAMILY: Sweet Potato (not botanically related to Yam), Morning Glory

MOSCHATEL (ADOXACEAE) FAMILY: Elderberry (varieties with red fruit must be cooked)

MULBERRY (MORACEAE) FAMILY: Breadfruit, Fig, Mulberry

MUSTARD (BRASSICACRAE/CRUCIFERAE) FAMILY: Bok Choy, Broccoli, Brussels Sprouts, Cauliflower, Chinese Cabbage, Collards, Common Cabbage, Kale, Kohlrabi, Horseradish, Mustard, Radish, Rapeseed (Canola Oil), Rutabaga, Sauerkraut, Savoy Cabbage, Seakale, Turnip, Wasabi, Watercress

MYRTLE (MYRLACEAE) FAMILY: Guava, Allspice, Clove, Vinca, Periwinkle

NIGHTSHADE (SOLANACEAE) FAMILY: Alkaloidal Glucosides, Belladonna, Cayenne, Chile Peppers, Chinese Artichoke, Eggplant, Henbane, Jimson Weed, Mandrake, Paprika (Capsicum, "natural" or "beta carotene"), Peppers (Sweet and Hot all varieties), Petunia, Pimiento, Potato, Scopalamine (sedative used in surgery and obstetrics), Tobacco, Tomatillo, Tomato. (Black peppercorns are NOT a Nightshade.)

NUTMEG (MYRISTICACEAE) FAMILY: Nutmeg (seed of fruit), Mace (tissue around fruit)

OLIVE (OLEACEAE) FAMILY: Ash, Forsythia, Jasmine, Lilac, Olive

ORCHID (ORCHIDACEAE) FAMILY: Orchid, Vanilla

PALM (ARECACEAE) FAMILY: Coconut, Sago Palm (source of Vitamin C), Date, Date Sugar, Palm Kernel Oil

PAPAYA (CARICACEAE) FAMILY: Papaya, Papain (used as a tenderizer for meat)

PARSLEY (APIACEAE) FAMILY: Angelica, Anise, Asafoetida, Caraway, Carrots, Celery, Celeriac, Celery Seed, Chervil, Coriander, Cumin, Dill, Fennel, Gotu Kola, Lovage, Parsley, Parsnip, Pennywort, Poison Hemlock, Sea Holly, Sweet Cicily, Water Celery

PAW PAW (ANNONACEAE) FAMILY: American Pawpaw, Cherimoya, Custard-Apple, Kentucky Banana, Ozark Banana, Prairie Banana, Soursop, Sweetsop

PEPPER (PIPERACEAE) FAMILY: Black, Green, Pink, White Peppercorns (Buckwheat hulls often used as filler in commercial ground pepper). Peppercorns are NOT part of the Nightshade Family.

PINE (PINACEAE) FAMILY: Pignoli, Pine Nuts (from North American pines), Capers (the pickled nut of a Mediterranean pine). Trivia: Pinocchio means Pine Nut in Italian.

PINEAPPLE (BROMELIACEAE) FAMILY: Ananas, Bromeliad, Pineapple

POMEGRANATE (LYTHRACEAE) FAMILY: Pomegranate, Rimmon

POPPY (PAPAVERACEAE) FAMILY: Heroin, Morphine, Opium, Poppy Seeds

PROTEA (PROTEACEAE) FAMILY: Macadamia Nut

ROSE (ROSACEAE) FAMILY: Rose Hips - APPLE SUBFAMILY: Asian Pear, Apple, Apple Cider and Vinegar, Apple Pectin, Crab Apple, Loquat, Pear, Quince - BERRY SUBFAMILY: Blackberry, Boysenberry, Currant, Dewberry, Gooseberry, Loganberry, Raspberry, Strawberry - PRUNE SUBFAMILY: Almond, Apricot, Black Cherry, Nectarine, Peach, Plum, Prune, Sour Cherry, Umeboshi plum (fruit and vinegar)

Note: Avoid honey from plants to which you are sensitive. Example: Tupelo Honey is from the blossoms of Dogwood trees, etc. Avoid sprouts from seeds, beans and grain to which you are sensitive. Example: Bean sprouts used in Chinese stir fry are from Mung beans. Avoid alcoholic beverages made from grains, potatoes and sugar if you are sensitive to them. Example: Scotch is made from barley.

Food Families

SEA VEGETABLES (PALMARIACEAE) FAMILY : Agar Agar, Arame, Blue Green Algae, Dulse, Hijiki, Kelp, Kombu, Nori, Spirulina, Wakame, etc. Sea Vegetables fall into three sub-families and are related to cabbage.

SEDGE (CYPERACEAE) FAMILY: Chinese Water Chestnut (plant not a tree nut), Water Caltrop, Chinese Sedge

SESAME (PEDALIACEA) FAMILY: Abongra, Benne seed, Sesame Seed, Sesame Oil, Sim Sim, Tahini, Til

SOAPBERRY (SAPINDACEAE) FAMILY: Litchi Nut, Lychee Nut, Saponin (a natural detergent)

SOURWOOD (POLYGONACEAE) FAMILY: Sorrel, Spinach Dock

SPURGE (EUPHORBIOIDEAE) FAMILY: Cassava, Manioc, Tapioca

SUCCULENT (AGAVACEAE) FAMILY: Agave, Tequila, Yucca - ASPHODELACEAE: Aloe

SUMAC (ANACARDIACEAE) FAMILY: Cashew Nut, Mango, Pistachio Nut, Poison Ivy, Poison Sumac

TEA (THEACEAE) FAMILY: Black Tea, Green Tea, Oolong, Orange Pekoe, Tea Tree Oil, White Tea, (Not Herb Tea)

WALNUT (JUGLANDACEAE) FAMILY: Black/English/White Walnuts, Butternut, Pecans, Hickory

YAM (DIASCOREACEAE) FAMILY: Chinese Yam, Indian Yam, Dioscorea opposita, Dioscorea polystachya (used to balance hormones), Wild Yam (Yam is not botanically related to the Sweet Potato)

NOTE: HONEY is a sweet viscid material elaborated out of the nectar of flowers in the honey sac of various Honeybees (Apidae Family). "The definition of honey stipulates a pure product that does not allow for the addition of any other substance. This includes, but is not limited to, water or other sweeteners." Look for raw, unprocessed locally produced honey. Other products produced by bees; Propolis, Royal Jelly, Wax

ANIMAL (ANIMALIA) KINGDOM

MOLLUSKS - PHYLUM MOLLUSCA
A large phylum of invertebrate animals with a non-segmented body enclosed in a shell.

ABALONE (HALIOTIDAE) FAMILY: Red, Pink and Green Abalone

CLAM (SPHAERIIDAE) FAMILY: Clams all varieties, Butter, Geoduck, Hard-Shell, Quahog, Pismo, Soft-Shell

COCKLE (CARDIIDAE) FAMILY: Cockle

MUSSEL (MYTILIDAE) FAMILY: Mussels

OYSTER (OSTREIDAE) FAMILY: Oyster all varieties

SCALLOP (PECTINIDAE) FAMILY: Sea Scallop, Bay Scallop

SNAIL (ENIDAE) FAMILY: Escargot, Slugs, Snails

SQUID (LOLIGINIDAE) FAMILY: Calamari, Cuttlefish, Octopus, Squid

CRUSTACEAN – ARTHROPODIA
A large class of arthropod having a crust or shell exoskeleton.

CRAB (CANCRIDAE) FAMILY: Crab all edible varieties hard and soft shell, Blue, European, Dungeness

LOBSTER (NEPHROPIDAE) FAMILY: Crayfish, Lobster all edible varieties, Rock Lobster

SHRIMP (PENAEIDAE) FAMILY: Shrimp all edible varieties, Prawn

VERTEBRATES – CARTILAGINOUS & BONY FISH
Fish with an internal skeletal structure and gills.
SW – Indicates Salt Water
FW – Indicates Fresh Water

fw BUFFALO FISH (CATOSTOMIDAE) FAMILY: Bigmouth and Black Buffalo, Sucker

fw CARP (CYPRINIDAE) FAMILY: Carp, Catfish, European Sea Bream, Yellow Bullhead (bottom feeders found in sluggish fresh water)

sw COD (GADIDAE) FAMILY: Atlantic Cod, Cod, Grayfish, Haddock, Pollack, Silver Hake, Tomcod, Whiting

sw CONGER EEL (CONGRIDAE) FAMILY: Conger Eel

fw/sw CROAKER (SCIAENIDAE) FAMILY: Atlantic Croaker, Freshwater Drumfish, King Whiting, Weakfish

sw DOLPHINFISH (CORYPHAENIDAE) FAMILY: Dolphinfish, Dorado, Mahi-mahi (family unrelated to Dolphins)

fw/sw EEL (ANGUILLIFORMES ORDER): Eel Common European and North American

sw FLOUNDER (PLEURONECTIFORMES) FAMILY: Flounder (Southern, Summer and Winter), Halibut (Atlantic and Pacific), Plaice, Sole, Turbot

fw/sw GRUNT (HAEMULIDAE) FAMILY: Grunt Common and Gray

sw HERRING (CLUPEIDAE) FAMILY: Anchovy, Herring Atlantic and Pacific, Sardines, Shad, Menhaden

fw/sw MULLET (MUGILIDAE) FAMILY: Fresh Water Minnows, Mullet; Gray, Stripped and White, Sllversides, White Bait

fw PADDLEFISH (POLYODONTIDAE) FAMILY: North American Paddlefish, Spoonbill, Spoonbill Catfish

fw/sw PERCH (PERCIFORMES) ORDER: FRESH WATER BASS (PERCIFORMES ORDER): Bass, Bluegill, Guadalullpe Bass, Largemouth Bass, Longeared Sunfish, Pumpkinseed, Rock Bass, Smallmouth Bass, Spotted Black Bass, Striped Bass, Sunfish - SEA BASS (SERRANIDAE) FAMILY; Butterfish, Sea Bass (Striped, White, Oriental Spotted, Smallmouth, Spotted Guadalupe, Yellow, and all varieties), Cogia, Croaker, Drum Fish, Grouper (Red and Brown), Grunt, Hind (Red and Speckled), Red Snapper, Rockfish, Sauger, Sheephead - TEMPERATE BASS (MORONIDAE) FAMILY; White Perch - PERCH (PERCIDAE) FAMILY; European Perch, Ocean Perch, Pike, Rosefish, Yellow Perch, Walleye Pike

Food Families

fw PIKE (ESOCIDAE) FAMILY: Northern Pike, Muskellunge

sw PORGY (SPARIDAE) FAMILY: Porgy, Scup

sw PUFFER (TETRAODONTIDAE) FAMILY: Balloonfish, Blowfish, Globefish, Puffer, Swellfish (eyes & organs toxic)

fw/sw SALMON (SALMONIDAE) FAMILY: Salmon all varieties: Atlantic, Pink, Sockeye, Coho, Dog and King Salmon, Trout; Brown, Rainbow, Brook and Lake, Whitefish, also Caviar from

sw SHARK (CHONDRICHTHYES CLASS) FAMILY: Dogfish, Ray all types, Skate, Shark all types

fw/sw SMELT (OSMERIDAE) FAMILY: Smelt (often used to garnish Sushi)

sw SOLE (SOLEOIDEI) FAMILY: Common Sole, Dover Sole, European Sole

fw STURGEON (ACIPENSERIDAE) FAMILY: Beluga, Caviar from, Sturgeon all varieties; Black and Caspian and North American Lake, Common, Russian,

sw TARPON (MEGALOPIDAE) FAMILY: Atlantic Tarpon, Pacific Tarpon

sw TUNA (SCOMBRIDAE) FAMILY: Ahi Ahi, Aku, Albacore, Amberjack, Bonito Atlantic and Chili, Bluefin, Bluefish, Bigeye, Butterfish, Mackerel Frigate, Jack and King, Mahi Mahi, Skipjack, Tunafish all varieties, Victorfish, Yellowfin

Even if you are not allergic to fish, use caution when purchasing. Because of the polluting of Earth's water, most fish have become unsafe for consumption. However, wild caught, small, cold water fish, eaten no more than three times per week, may be tolerated better than larger fatty fish. (Large oily fish have more years to become contaminated and the "bad" stuff collects in the fat, as it does with all creatures).

Fish raised in farms may not be safe unless the feed they are given is organic. Be suspicious of all commercially-produced food. I do not promote the consumption or use of pork, crustacean, fish without scales, dairy, alcohol, coffee, chocolate, marijuana, opium or any exotic wildlife. However, depending on the source and/or severity of your allergies, I have made the information available to you. As a general rule, eat low on the food chain to eliminate as many pollutants, hormones, preservatives, antibiotics and pesticides as possible. Keep in mind that most toxins are stored in animal fat — all animals! If you eat meat, eat it minimally-processed and as natural as possible.

AMPHIBIANS
Cold-blooded vertebrates with wet skin.

FROG (ANURA) FAMILY: American and European Edible Bullfrog

BIRDS
Warm blooded vertebrate with wings and feathers.

CHICKEN (PHASIANIDAE) FAMILY: Chicken, Cornish Hen, Guinea fowl, Peafowl, Pheasant Domestic and Indian, Quail, also the livers and eggs of all varieties

DOVE (COLUMBIDAE) FAMILY: Dove, Pigeon, also the livers and eggs of all varieties

DUCK (ANATIDAE) FAMILY: Duck, Geese, Swan. and Goose, also the livers and eggs of all varieties

GROUSE (TETRAONIDAE) FAMILY: Grouse, Prairie Chicken, also the livers and eggs of all varieties

TURKEY (MELEAGRIDIDAE) FAMILY: Turkey Domestic and Wild, also the livers and eggs of all varieties

MAMMALS
Warm-blooded vertebrate with hair, who nourish their young with milk.

BEAVER (CASTORIDAE) FAMILY: Beaver

BOVINE (BOVIDAE) FAMILY: American Bison, Brahman, Buffalo, Cattle, Cow (Beef, Butter, Buttermilk, Casein, Cheese, Cow Milk, Dairy, Ghee (considered gluten and casein-free),
Kefir, Gelatin, Goat (Goat Milk, Cheese), Longhorn Steer, Rennin, Sausage Casing, Veal, Whey, Yogurt, etc.), Sheep (Lamb, Mutton)

DEER (CERVIDAE) FAMILY: American Elk, European Red and White Tailed Deer (Venison), Caribou, Moose, Reindeer

HORSE (EQUIDAE) FAMILY: Ass, Donkey, Horse, Onager, Zebra

MUSKRAT (CRICETIDAE) FAMILY: Hamster, Lemming, Muskrat, Vole

OPOSSUM (DIDELPHIDAE) FAMILY: Opossum

RABBIT (LEPORIDAE) FAMILY: Cottontail Eastern and Western, Hare, Pika, Rabbit Domestic, Jack and Snowshoe

SQUIRREL (SCIURIDAE) FAMILY: Squirrel all varieties, Marmots, Prairie Dog, Woodchuck

SWINE (SUIDAE) FAMILY: Pig (Bacon, Ham, Lard, Pork, Sausage, etc.), Swine, Wild Boar, Worthog

NOTE: Always choose meats that are minimally processed, antibiotic free and hormone free.

By Any Other Name

ere is a short list of other names that food manufacturers use to refer to common foods and some foods they are in. Hopefully, this will help you with your new hobby — label reading.

Restricted Foods	May Be Listed On Label As	Foods To Avoid
MILK & DAIRY	Casein Caseinate Whey Lactalbumin Sodium caseinate Lactose Non-fat milk solids Cream Calcium caseinate	Cheese Cottage cheese Ice cream, yogurt Creamed soups & sauces Butter & most margarines Baked goods made with milk Some "non-dairy" products Candy (cream & milk chocolate) Custards & puddings
EGG	Albumin Egg whites Egg yolks	Many baked goods Egg noodles Custards & puddings Mayonnaise, some salad dressings Hollandaise sauce Meringues Many egg substitutes (Egg-beaters) Some batter-fried foods
WHEAT	(Enriched) flour Wheat germ Wheat bran Wheat starch Gluten Food Starch Vegetable starch Vegetable gum Duram Semolina Starch Solids	Many baked goods made with wheat flour Crackers Macaroni, Spaghetti, Noodles Gravies, thickened sauces Fried food coating Baking mixes Soy sauce Hot dogs with wheat filler Batter fried foods Some sausages Rye bread, Corn bread
BEEF	Shortening Lard Gelatin	Soups Bouillon Beef gravies and sauces Hot dogs
PORK	Shortening Lard	Cold cuts Bacon Sausage Hot dogs Baked beans and soups with pork

Keep in mind that thousands of different ingredients are not required by law to be listed on the label. Ask yourself, how many different hands have touched the food before it reaches your table?

Restricted Foods	May Be Listed On Label As	Foods To Avoid
SOY	Soy flour Soybean oil Vegetable oil Soy protein Soy protein isolate Textured vegetable protein (TVP) Vegetable starch Vegetable gum	Soy sauce Teriyaki sauce Worcestershire sauce Tuna packed in vegetable oil Tofu Baked goods or cereals that include soy Soy nuts Soy infant formulas (Isomil, Prosobee) Most margarines
CORN	Cornmeal Corn starch Corn oil Corn syrup (solids) Corn sweetener Corn alcohol Vegetable oil Vegetable starch Vegetable gum Food starch	Some baked goods Corn tortillas (chips, tacos) Popcorn Some cold cereals Corn syrup Pancake syrup Many candies Most baking powders Tofu Some vitamins
CHOCOLATE	Cocoa Cocoa butter	Candy Baked goods Colas

A word about some food items: Some brands of baking soda may contain trace amounts of gluten. Most vitamin C crystals are made from a non-allergic corn source. Barley malt (gluten) is used in the process of some rice and soy beverages. Corn is used in some brands of tofu. Call the individual manufacture to be sure. Only you know how strict you need to be. Did you know hydrolyzed vegetable protein is not currently considered a food additive, usually made up of soy protein broken down into amino acids - one of which is glutamic acid. HVP, according to the book "Hard to Swallow - the Truth About Food Additives", is the main ingredient for MSG monosodium glutamate. HVP may contain up to 40% MSG. ■

Sugar By Any Other Name

feel so strongly about avoiding sugar that I am devoting an entire page to the subject. Sugar, in my opinion, is the gateway drug. Most alcoholics and drug users also have a sweet tooth. Unused sugar ferments in our gut and cause people to actually behave as if they are drunk or high. Anyone who has ever taught school age children knows that the day after Halloween is pandemonium in the classroom. Too much sugar rots teeth, causes dramatic sugar highs and lows and creates an acid pH in body systems.

Added sugars in processed foods can be found under the following names:

Sugar (sucrose) - the refined crystallized sugar; a combination of glucose and fructose.

Dextrose (glucose) - a simple sugar made of only one molecule.

Lactose - a simple sugar from milk.

Maltose - a simple sugar made from starch, usually grains.

Maltodextrin - a manufactured sugar from maltose and dextrose; usually from corn.

Brown sugar - the refined sugar coated with molasses or colored with caramel.

Raw sugar - a less refined sugar with a small amount of molasses remaining.

Fructose - a simple sugar refined from fruit.

Corn syrup - a manufactured syrup of corn starch, containing varying proportions of glucose, maltose, and dextrose.

High-fructose corn syrup - a highly concentrated syrup of predominantly fructose.

White grape juice - a highly purified fructose solution; virtually no other nutrients are present.

Be aware: cornstarch treated by heat or enzymes to make dextrose, maltose, corn syrup, corn sugar, and crystalline dextrose, is used to supplement sucrose in processed foods in order to bring costs down, add color and flavor, and retain bright colors in preserves, ketchup and cured meat. This widespread use may be a cause of the increased allergies to corn.

Typically, when ingredients are listed on a product, they must be listed from largest amount down to smallest amount. Do not be fooled into thinking there is very little sugar in an item if it is not listed near the beginning. Often you will find three or four of the above aliases in the ingredient listing, meaning that in the end the product may be mostly sugar! When reading a label, note the grams of sugar per serving, then look at the serving size. For example a 20 ounce bottle of Classic Coke has 27 grams of sugar per serving and the bottle contains two-and-a-half servings. That means that the bottle has a total of 67.5 grams of sugar, not 27.

When salt is iodized, some type of sugar must be added to keep the salt from clumping. High-glycemic foods that turn to sugar rapidly are: white potato, white rice, white flour, pasta, white bread, bananas, dairy in all forms, fruit juice, alcohol, oranges and grapes. Excess sugar consumed in a meal is converted into fat for use another time. Fermented sugars in the blood stream are food for parasites, viruses and bacteria. We are addicted to sugar because all food is converted into sugar. It is what our brain uses for fuel. Of course we crave it. The question is about the quality of the fuel. I have known heroin users who said it was easier to give up the heroin than the craving for sugar.

Choose foods that convert slowly into sugar for long lasting energy. You guessed it — vegetables, whole grains, nuts, beans and seeds. Popeye didn't eat a candy bar for energy — he ate spinach! ■

Acid/Alkaline-Forming Foods

There are two ways of looking at the acid or alkaline values of foods. One is to measure how acid or how alkaline the foods themselves may be. The other is how the food changes the pH value of the tissues or their acid or alkaline-forming ability on the body. Once the food is digested, an "ash" is formed. The pH of this ash can be quite different than the actual pH value of the food. A good example would be lemons. The actual lemon is very acidic, however, once digested, lemon has a very alkalizing effect. To say it differently, the pH condition foods cause in the body after being digested is the one that will be the focus in changing the body's pH. I will give you a hint — think green!

The pH of foods will change, usually becoming more acid when cooked. Eat fruits and vegetables fresh, organic and raw whenever possible for maximum benefit. If poor digestion, bloating and gas occur, lightly steam produce until your body becomes more in-balance and accustomed to your new healthier way of eating and living.

Highly Alkaline-Forming Foods

Almond raw, artichokes, arugula, asparagus, avocado, baking soda, beet greens, beet red, broccoli, cabbage green, cabbage lettuce, cabbage red, cabbage savoy, cabbage white, carrot, cauliflower, celery, celery root, chard, chicory, chlorella, chives, cilantro, collards, comfrey, cucumber, dandelion greens, eggplant, endive, fennel, garlic, ginger, grass wheat and it's fresh juice (and most edible grasses such as barley, kamut and their juices), green beans, jicama, kohlrabi, leeks, lemon, lettuce romaine, lettuce leaf all variety, lettuce lamb's, lima beans, lime, lotus root, mineral water, mustard greens, onion green, onion stored, parsley, peas fresh, pepper sweet and hot all

www.feelgoodfood.com

varieties, pumpkin, radish horse, radish summer black, radish red, rhubarb stalks unsweetened, rutabaga, sea salt, sea vegetables, seaweed, sorrel, soy lecithin pure, soy beans fresh, soy nuts air dried, spinach, sprouted beans-grains-seeds all edible varieties, squash hard varieties, summer squash, sweet potato, taro root, tomato, tomatillo, turnip, umeboshi plums, wasabi, watercress, zucchini.

Moderately Alkaline-Forming Foods

Borage oil, brazil nut raw, buckwheat groats, burdock root, caraway seeds, chia seeds, cumin seeds, dasheen, fennel seeds, flax seed oil, flax seeds raw, hazelnut raw, herbs fresh, millet, nigella seeds, parsnip, poppy seeds, pumpkin seeds raw, radish white, rutabaga, sesame seeds raw, soy flour, stevia, sweet potato raw, sunflower seeds raw, tofu.

Low Alkaline-Forming Foods

Apple, apricot, banana, black currant, blueberry, cantaloupe, cherry sweet, cherry tart, cold-pressed oils fresh, currant, date, evening primrose oil, fig fresh, flax seed oil expeller pressed, gooseberry ripe, grape, grapefruit, kiwi, mandarin orange, mango, marine lipids, nectarine, olive oil expeller pressed, orange, papaya, peach, pear, pineapple, plum Italian, plum yellow, pomegranate, raspberry, red currant, rosehips, strawberry, tangerine, ugli fruit, watermelon.

NOTE: Because of the high sugar content of sweet fruit, whole fruits listed are best in season, for cleansing purposes or in moderation only.

Very Low Alkaline-Forming Foods

Amaranth, black-eyed peas, Bragg Liquid Aminos™, carob, fava beans, head lettuce, herbs dried non-irradiated, kamut, miso, mushrooms, pecans, quinoa, rice basmati, rice brown, spelt, spices dried non-irradiated, string bean, sunflower oil expeller pressed, teff, vegetable broth natural packaged, vegetables cooked, walnuts, wax beans, wild rice.

Neutral (near/neutral) Ash Foods

Butter organic, coconut meat & water fresh, ghee, milk raw unpasteurized from hormone and antibiotic free cows, most expeller pressed oils not already listed, water pure source not tap, yogurt raw unpasteurized, Xylitol (the pH of saliva and plaque does not fall with xylitol).

Very Low Acid-Forming Foods

Agave nectar, brown rice syrup, corn fresh, cream, fish fresh water such as salmon, fruit cooked or dried, date sugar, fruit juice natural packaged, honey raw unpasteurized, lentils, liver, milk homogenized, olives green and ripe, organ meats, oysters, rye bread, soft goat and cow cheeses, sprouted-grain bread and meal, whole-grain bread and meal.

Acid/Alkaline-Forming Foods

Low Acid-Forming Food

Barley, beans dried, carob, cashews, cheese hard aged, corn oil, cranberry, fructose, granola, legume dried, milk sugar, peanuts, pistachios, Sucanat (tm), sugar turbinado, soybeans processed, soy sauce, tamari, tapioca, vanilla, wheat, white potatoes stored.

Moderately Acid-Forming Food

Bacon, barley Malt Sweetener, beef, biscuit white, bread white, chicken, eggs, cakes, corn meal, crab, lobster, macaroni whole grain & cheese organic, oatmeal, oats, ocean fish, pasta, pastries, pork, rice white, sausages, shrimp, turkey, veal.

Highly Acid-Forming Foods

Alcohol all types including beer and wine, artificial sweeteners (NutraSweet, Spoonful, Sweet 'N Low, Equal or Aspartame), candy, cheese processed, cocoa, coffee, cottonseed oil, cow's milk that has been homogenized and pasteurized, fried foods all types, game birds, hydrogenated oil, ice cream, jam, jelly, hops, malt, margarine, milk chocolate, MSG, processed foods, pudding, sugar processed white all types, table salt (NaCl), vegetable oil super heated, vinegar white (acetic acid), yeast — and all soft drinks, especially the cola type. To neutralize a glass of cola with a pH of 2.8, it would take 32 glasses of alkaline water with a pH of 7.0.

A Final Thought on pH Balance

It isn't just foods that make us acid. Most prescription medications and over-the-counter drugs may be highly acid as well. Check with your doctor. Recreational drugs are also highly acid-forming.

Just as Toxic Thoughts are Acid so are Overwork, Anger, Fear, Jealousy and Stress. To become more Alkaline try Positive Thought, Meditation, Prayer, Peace, Kindness and Love. ■

NOTE: The above foods are listed in alphabetical order within the main headings - NOT in the order of their pH forming ability. Be sure to enjoy foods being mindful of; variety, moderation and consistency. For best results, it is recommended that total avoidance of all foods in the Moderately and Highly Acid-Forming Foods categories be observed, and that the majority of food choices be made out of the Highly and Moderately Alkaline-Forming categories for optimum pH balance.

Food Combining

One food at a meal is ideal! The safest way to eat on a daily basis is to eat simply. It is helpful to keep a log of everything you eat and are around. Once you have your health under control and feel comfortable with this new way of eating, add in more recipes and ideas. In time you will have your own program. Drink half your body weight in ounces of water from a pure source a day, but never with food. Your goal is to aid digestion not slow it down. Take it slow and be forgiving when you make mistakes.

> NOTE: Any combination of vegetables may be mixed with either one protein or one starch per meal. Sweet fruits should never follow or be eaten with a protein, starch or vegetable.

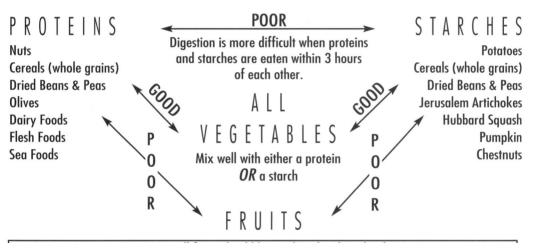

PROTEINS

Nuts
Cereals (whole grains)
Dried Beans & Peas
Olives
Dairy Foods
Flesh Foods
Sea Foods

POOR
Digestion is more difficult when proteins and starches are eaten within 3 hours of each other.

GOOD

ALL VEGETABLES
Mix well with either a protein *OR* a starch

GOOD

POOR

POOR

FRUITS

STARCHES

Potatoes
Cereals (whole grains)
Dried Beans & Peas
Jerusalem Artichokes
Hubbard Squash
Pumpkin
Chestnuts

> NOTE: Not all fruits should be combined with each other.
> Eat fruit at least 1/2 hour before other foods never with or after a meal.

ACID ← Poor → SUB-ACID ← Poor → SWEET

ACID	SUB-ACID	SWEET
Citrus Fruits	Apples	Bananas
Pineapples	Apricots	Dates
Plums (sour)	Cherries	Figs
Pomegranates	Grapes	Prunes
Strawberries	Mangos	Raisins
Berries	Papayas	Persimmons
Sour Fruits	Pears	

EXCEPTIONS

Avocado – combines well with all foods except proteins and melons
Tomatoes – may be eaten with non-starchy vegetables and protein
Melons – eat them alone or leave them alone

Tools

Tools are one of the things that separate us from other animals. In a healthy safe kitchen, the proper tools will separate you from drudgery and ill health. Everyone has their own style, only you know what yours is. Some will want to test the waters first and use up what they already have, others will plunge in headfirst and get rid of everything and start fresh. If you are like me you will be somewhere in the middle. Care packages of food went to neighbors, friends and family, while pots and pans were slowly changed. Budget will be another factor. Not everyone can afford to replace everything in their kitchen in a weekend. I pride myself in being a practical person; never do anything that throws your life out of balance. The following suggestions are just that, suggestions — they have made my life easier, so I will pass them along to you.

Glass

Glass is the best and safest for many cooking needs. Saucepans and baking dishes should always be glass. Also, glass makes the best freezing containers. I have sets of glass nesting bowls with plastic lids (make sure the lid does not touch the food). If you live in an area that has outlet stores, look for one that carries these items. It is a great way to pick up a bargain. If not, buy a set at a time until you have what you need. Never store food in plastic; it will leach into the once safe food and make it unsafe. Your bottled drinking water should always be stored in glass. Also, never place food in a thermos bottle lined with plastic. You may need to make an exception for food being packed for children.

Stainless Steel

Stainless Steel is my choice for frying pans and large pots. Good copper clad stainless steel is worth the investment and will last a life time. Non-stick coatings have been known to emit harmful vapors and should be avoided. Waffle irons may be the only exception. While a non-stick coating is not ideal, it is the only way I have found to keep the batter from bonding to the iron. If this is a concern for you, don't make waffles. Never use aluminum, iron, copper, etc. These metals are porous and will leach into the food, adding extras your body does not need. Never store food in aluminum foil or plastic.

Blender

If you invest in nothing else buy a GOOD blender. I use mine every day. Soups, sauces, batters, shakes, dressings, puddings, you name it and I've made it in my blender. Make sure it has a strong motor, stainless steel blades, and cleans easily (dishwasher safe is a big plus). I use a Vita Mix (which doubles as a juicer and can make flour from whole grains). When blending anything hot be sure to leave air space to allow steam to escape and prevent getting burned by exploding liquid.

Food Processor

A Food Processor is not necessary, but a real time saver. Chapati, crackers, sorbet, chopped and shredded vegetables, chopped nuts, and most importantly large batches can be made in a matter of seconds. A food processor will cut hours off of your time in the kitchen. Make sure it has a strong motor and is dishwasher safe. When you add up all the money you save by not going to fast food restaurants or on cookies, ice cream and junk-food, in no time a processor will more than pay for itself.

Juicer

A Juicer is also not a necessity, but nice to have. There is nothing like a glass of fresh carrot juice with a lemon twist and a stalk of celery before dinner. There are products on the market that combine the functions of a blender, juicer and processor along with some other features, shop around and find the best one for your needs.

Baking Stone

Baking stones, the best (in my opinion) for crackers, cookies and pizzas. a good way to avoid aluminum cookie sheets.

Knives

If you invest in nothing else buy a really good set of knives, they will last a lifetime.

Tools

Gadgets

Pizza Wheel, perfect for cutting pancakes.

Wire Whisk, a must for thin batters.

Apple Corer, aside from the obvious, core a cucumber stuff a carrot in the hole and cut into slices, serve with lunch in place of potato chips, even fussy kids will eat these.

Wooden Craft Sticks, turn juice or sorbet into a popsicle. Can't eat a bun with your minimally processed hot dog?. . eat it on a stick, kids love it!

Melon Baller, the perfect way to remove the seeds and /or the centers of pears, apples and other fruits. Perfect for onions and other veggies for stuffing.

Pepper Mill, great way to grind whole cloves, nutmeg, mustard seed, etc.

Electric Coffee Grinder, excellent way to grind seeds and nuts into a fine powder. Sucanat can be turned into powdered sugar and teff seed can be ground to a flour.

Electric Rice Steamer, wonderful time saver. A steamer will make eating your veggie based meals a healthy "fast food" experience.

Quick Defrost Tray, space age material which draws the cold away from frozen food. Defrosts more efficiently than a microwave.

Mandolin Slicer, makes shoestring carrots, garnishes and more. Look for brands that are durable and include a slicer, chopper, grater/slicer and zester/shredder. Make sure it has a stainless steel cutting blade. This tool will make you look like a pro.

Vegetable Steamer, healthiest way to lightly steam vegetables. Nutrients don't boil away in the water. ■

Breakfast

Breakfast Ideas

The toughest meal for most people is breakfast. We want breakfast to be a "no brainer" — quick, easy and a jump start on the day. If, like most Americans, you've been starting off your day with coffee or a cola beverage and maybe a pop tart or cold cereal, to say the least, this new way is going to be tough. Especially if you feel sick, tired, work five days a week and are getting the kids and husband off to school and work. This new routine might be tough, but not impossible especially when you see the results.

Your own personal style will determine your exact routine. Here is one possible scenario; Before brushing your teeth (with your new fluoride free health food store toothpaste), eat your (rotationally correct, fist sized) piece of fruit or your wheat, barley and kamut grass drink. You may need to allow an additional fifteen minutes or so to prepare breakfast and lunch for the day. Do what you can the night before such as making an extra portion at dinner and eating that for breakfast or to pack for lunch. Better yet slice an avocado and mix it into Breakfast Salad page 48 and really start the day off right. Since you have had your piece of fruit or green drink early morning, breakfast can be brought along and eaten at your first break of the day. Only you can determine what will work. Experiment and be sure to laugh at the situation.

Perhaps the easiest way to start might be to try this new way of looking at food one or two mornings a week and add days until you feel comfortable. The best advice I can give is to keep it SIMPLE! The modern world we live in is complicated and stress filled enough. More stress is not your goal.

Organic fresh greens are best, but vegetable soup or a baked sweet potato makes a great breakfast on cold mornings too. Think of as many non-traditional ideas as possible. Also if you are following a strict food combining program, make choices from the foods allowed for that day. Be intuitive and ingenious and make this work for you.

Breakfast Ideas

I have started a list, please add foods that work for you!

Glass of Water with Fresh Squeezed Lemon

Sliced Avocados

Fresh Green Salad

Gogi Berry & Almond Trail Mix

Wheat, Barley & Kamut Grass Drink Gluten-Free

Cream of Buckwheat - Gluten-Free

Quinoa Flakes - Gluten-Free

Brown Rice with Rice Milk - Gluten-Free

Whole Grain Amaranth - Gluten-Free

Steamed Vegetables

Raw Vegetables

Vegetable Soup

Baked Sweet Potato

Pancakes & Waffles

I f you crave a more traditional breakfast or snack, these wheat, egg, dairy and sugar-free pancakes and waffles are for you. I tried three different waffle irons before I found one that works. I never give up when it comes to food! Without the eggs, nothing seemed to keep the batter from bonding like glue to the waffle iron, even non-stick surfaces. I have since found that a Belgian Waffle Iron works best. When frozen, these waffles can make a quick breakfast popped in the toaster. The pancakes thaw quickly when heated in a dry skillet.

5 MINUTES TO PREPARE BATTER

SEE RECIPE, TIME TO COOK VARIES

BELGIAN WAFFLE IRON OR GRIDDLE

STOVE TOP METHOD

SEE RECIPE FOR NUMBER OF

CAKES / WAFFLES

VARIATIONS

- One half cup chopped nuts, carob chips, vegetables, fruit or herbs may be added to the batter depending on your purpose. Mince fine for waffles.
- Pour batter with chopped veggies in muffin pan and bake 30 minutes in a 350° oven.
- Add stevia to taste, for a sweet batter.
- Thin the batter and make crepe's, fill with fruit or veggies.
- For a quick treat, alternate layers of pancakes with almond butter. Cut into wedges and serve.
- Use Candida Safe Syrup, page 167.
-

Batter Ingredients

QUINOA - GLUTEN-FREE

- 1-1/2 cups Quinoa flour
- 1/2 cup Tapioca flour
- 1/2 teaspoon Baking Soda
- 1/2 teaspoon Vitamin C Crystals
- 1/2 teaspoon Sea Salt (optional)
- 1 teaspoon ground Nutmeg
- 3 tablespoons Sunflower oil
- 1-3/4 cups pure Water

AMARANTH - GLUTEN-FREE

- 1-1/2 cups Amaranth flour (one box)
- 1/2 cup Arrowroot starch
- 1/2 cup ground Hazel Nuts (Filbert)
- 1/2 teaspoon Baking Soda
- 1/2 teaspoon Vitamin C Crystals
- 1/2 teaspoon Sea Salt (optional)
- 3 tablespoons Canola oil
- 2 cups pure Water

SPELT or KAMUT - NON-HYBRID WHEAT

- 2 cups Spelt or Kamut flour
- 1/2 teaspoon Baking Powder
- 1/2 teaspoon Vitamin C Crystals
- 1/2 teaspoon Sea Salt (optional)
- 1 tsp ground Cinnamon (optional)
- 3 tbl. Light Olive or Walnut Oil
- 1 teaspoon Vanilla
- 2 cups pure Water

Note: If using a non-alcohol vanilla, increase amount to 1 tablespoon.

RICE - GLUTEN-FREE and/or
OAT - GLUTEN

- 1 cup each Rice & Oat flour or 2 cups Rice or Oat flour
- 1/2 teaspoon Baking Soda
- 1/2 teaspoon Vitamin C Crystals
- 1/2 teaspoon Sea Salt (optional)
- 3 tablespoons Almond** or Sesame oil or any light oil
- 2 cups gluten-free Rice beverage
- 1 teaspoon Vanilla
- 2 tablespoons Agar Agar
- 6 drops Stevia or sweeten to taste (optional)

BUCKWHEAT - GLUTEN-FREE

- 1-1/2 cups Buckwheat flour
- 1/2 cup Arrowroot Starch
- 1/2 teaspoon Baking Powder
- 1/2 teaspoon Sea Salt (optional)
- 1/2 teaspoon Vitamin C Crystals
- 3 tablespoons Canola oil
- 2 cups pure Water

**Note: Use different oil if allergic to almonds.

Batter Preparation

I n a large bowl combine all dry ingredients and mix by hand.
Next make a well in the center and add half of the liquid, add oil and start
bringing the flour into the well. Add remaining liquid and mix all together.

NOTE: Pancake batter will need to be on the thin side, however, if you are making waffles the batter should be thicker. Experience is the best teacher. If the batter seems too thin, add flour one tablespoon at a time; if too thick, do the same with the liquid. At this point add any other ingredients mentioned in the variation you have chosen. If you have the luxury of time, allow the batter to rest in the refrigerator an hour prior to cooking, when the batter is cold it will rise a little better, this step is nice but not necessary.

COOKING

Heat a heavy skillet/griddle or waffle iron. Lightly oil griddle (using same oil used in recipe), one application of oil is usually enough, but you are the best judge of sticking. For waffle iron follow the manufacturer's instructions. When a bead of water dances on surface you are ready to begin. This batter will not cook the same as wheat, egg, and milk batter, practice may be necessary before the desired results can be achieved. Do not give up! Once you master the correct techniques, the results will be wonderful. Start with small cakes until you become familiar with the different batters.

Cooking

PANCAKES

Start with one four inch cake in center of pan, size will depend on use. When entire surface bubbles lift one edge to see if bottom is lightly brown. Work around all edges until cake comes loose and flip, when second side is light brown remove to a plate. Amaranth will take twice as long to cook. If making crepes, batter should be thin and a 9" skillet or crepe pan is recommended, spelt and quinoa work best.

WAFFLES

Batter should be fairly thick. Sometimes if the waffle sticks it is because the batter is too thin. Another reason may be cooking time. I've found 3 to 4 minutes works with all of the batters except the Amaranth. Allow up to 8 minutes for Amaranth. If the waffle starts to split, it is not done cooking — allow more time! Gently loosen the corners and the waffle should pop out.

STORAGE

Place in a single layer on a cookie sheet and freeze. Once frozen, stack in a freezer safe container for another day. They may be thawed out in a toaster.

SERVING SUGGESTIONS

Even though these pancakes and waffles are acid-forming, they are what I consider to be "healthy acid-forming" and make a better choice for that 20% portion of your diet. Great side with our delicious Breakfast Salad — pages 48-49.

Note: These alternative flour will become rancid quickly if not kept refrigerated.

Sweet Breakfast Smoothies

Quick and easy, a great once-in-a-while start to the day or a mid-afternoon treat. One of these wonderful, healthful drinks will make a great start to your day. Smoothie recipes are everywhere, however, most of them call for yogurt or tofu as the creamy thickening agent.

I find that Frozen chunks of fruit thickens just fine. If you have not planned ahead use a cup of ice with fresh fruit. Children love shakes, and a smoothie should solve the nightmare of what to do in a rush before school without cold cereal and milk.

5 MINUTES TO PUT TOGETHER

BLENDER

FREEZER

VARIATIONS

- Any fruit or berry will work. Please don't mix melon with any other type of fruit or eat if you have a Candida overgrowth. Refer to the food combining chart, page 25.
- Any fresh squeezed juice or herb tea may be interchanged.
- Rice beverage, fresh almond milk may replace organic coconut milk.
- If fresh fruit is out of season, organic frozen is an excellent alternative.
- The herb stevia is worth searching for. It is the only natural sweetener I know of that will not cause a candida flair up. Although not candida safe, a tablespoon of agave nectar or a tablespoon or two of fruit juice concentrate will also work if any sweetener is even needed.

- _____

Ingredients

- 1 cup frozen Mango sections
- 1/2 cup chilled organic unsweetened Coconut Milk
- 1 fresh Lime – Juiced
- 6 drops Stevia or to desired sweetness
- 1/8 teaspoon Acidophilus (non-dairy)
- 1 tablespoon ground Flax
- (Optional) Whole food concentrate, such as, Juice Plus™ or VidaCell™

PREPARATION

CONSTANTS IN THE FORMULA: Something frozen to thicken the Smoothie: bananas, ice, juice or rice beverage in ice cube form, pineapple, etc. Non-dairy acidophilus (the good bacteria for your intestines) and flax, one of the best vegetarian sources of essential fatty acids found in nature — do not substitute.

VARIANTS IN THE FORMULA: Fruit, sweetener, juice and thickness. Place all ingredients in blender and blend starting on lowest setting and raising to highest a couple of minutes until contents are smooth and creamy, add extra water a little at a time until desired thickness is achieved.

SERVING SUGGESTIONS

Pour into popsicle forms and freeze.

Suitable for an ice cream maker. Make extra thick and eat with a spoon.

This is a better choice than a traditional "milk" shake for children of all ages.

Note: If you suffer from headaches, an allergy to Vasoactive amines may be the culprit. It is a chemical found in some foods including bananas, chocolate, ripened cheese, avocados, sausage (bologna, salami, hotdogs, etc.), chicken livers and yeast extracts. If you are not sure about these foods, omit them from your diet for four days and binge on them the fifth. You will have your answer. This method of testing for allergies works for most foods. Please check with your doctor first.

Carob Breakfast Pudding

I f you are looking for a hot stick to your ribs breakfast, look no further. This is so yummy you may want to eat it for dessert (I know I have). Whole grain teff may be used but I recommend using teff flour. Unfortunately, teff flour is not always available. However, if you have an electric coffee grinder sitting around gathering dust, pull it out, and dust it off — because it is the fastest and best way to turn whole teff into teff flour.

10 Minutes to Prepare

Sauce Pan

Stove Top

Serves Four

VARIATIONS

- Toss in 1/2 cup shredded unsweetened coconut.
- Cool and form into 1" balls and roll in raw honey then chopped nuts and or coconut, refrigerate and enjoy like fudge another time.
- Add extra stevia and use between layers of Carob Cake page 156.
- Use agave nectar, xylitol or maple syrup instead of honey. (Stevia is the best choice)
- _____
- _____

Ingredients

- 3/4 cup Teff flour, toasted · GLUTEN-FREE
- 1/2 cup Carob powder
- Pinch Sea Salt

- 2 cups pure Water or gluten-free Rice beverage. Add an additional 3 tablespoons if not using Honey

- 3 tablespoons Honey -or- 1/4 teaspoon liquid Stevia or to taste - or - Agave Nectar
- 1/4 cup chopped Pecans or Walnuts *(optional)*

PREPARATION

In a dry sauce pan toast teff until fragrant, about 2 minutes, stir constantly to prevent scorching. Add carob and salt, stir to mix. While still stirring, add water until well blended and there are no lumps. Bring to a boil, turn down heat and simmer 5 minutes, continue to stir occasionally, to prevent burning. Once thick, remove from heat and add honey or stevia to taste and nuts, stir to blend and serve at once.

SERVING SUGGESTIONS

A really good, densely nutritious "between salad" treat.

Serve pudding hot in a bowl, drench in rice or fresh almond milk and watch it disappear.

Makes a great after school treat when you use the 'fudge ball', as described in Variations page 38.

Note: Do not use honey or agave if on a candida diet.
Check to make sure the brand of rice beverage you use is gluten-free.

Blueberry Muffins

I put this recipe together for a client of ours at The Alternative (a nutrition consultation service where I was employed). The nutritionist I worked for asked me to help a long-time client kick the sugar 'habit'. Mentally she wanted to change nutritional habits of a lifetime, but the reality of the situation was she CRAVED sweets 24 hours a day and was miserable and guilty as a result. I also suggested she add a tablespoon of Sucanat™ or honey to start and cut back as she became used to the stevia. I know she is going to make it.

Oven Temperature 350°

20 Minutes to Prepare

30 – 35 Minutes to Bake

8 Regular or 24 Mini Muffins

Oil Muffin Tins, Lightly Flour

VARIATIONS

- Use orange zest in place of the lemon. Just about all fruit is coated in wax before or at market. Most of this wax is loaded with poisons and toxins, it may even be on your organic fruit! Be sure you are using a fruit and veggie rinse that is cutting through the wax.
- Use another berry or fruit in place of blueberries.
- If using spelt or kamut decrease amount of flour by 1/2 cup.
- This may also be made in a bread or cake pan and sliced.
- _____
- _____

Ingredients

- 2 cups Brown Rice flour · GLUTEN-FREE
- 3/4 cup Tapioca flour
- 1/2 tsp. each. Sea Salt, Baking Soda & Vitamin C Crystals
- Zest from one organic Lemon, with all wax removed.

- 1/4 teaspoon Stevia liquid to taste or 1/3 cup Agave Nectar
- 1 tablespoon Agar Agar
- 1 cup gluten-free Brown Rice beverage
- Juice from one Lemon
- 1/3 cup expeller pressed Grapeseed Oil or Canola Oil

- 1-1/2 cups fresh or frozen Blueberries

- Brown Rice flour and oil for muffin tins

PREPARATION

Soak agar in rice milk for 5 minutes. Mix all dry ingredients. Add all liquid ingredients to dry, stir liquid mixture in with dry mixture. Once combined, add the cup of blueberries, or cranberries, or chopped apples, or nuts, etc. Tip: Zest lemon before cutting or juicing.

Oil and generously flour muffin cups — do not use paper liners. The batter will be stiff — be sure to smooth tops, they will look the same cooked as they do uncooked. Bake in a preheated 350° oven for 30 - 35 minutes or until golden. Allow 30 minutes for muffins to set. Good warm or at room temperature. Makes 8 muffins.

SERVING SUGGESTIONS

Excellent way to introduce someone to the new gluten-free way of eating and enjoying life. Good as a side with our delicious Breakfast Salad — page 48-49.

* Note: Do not use honey if on a candida diet
** Note: If using a non-alcohol vanilla increase amount to 1 tablespoon.

Orange Muffins

Oranges used to be the only fruit that my youngest son was not allergic, (at one time he was allergic to all but ten foods). When I came up with this recipe, he was delighted. This is a dense sweet bread your whole family will enjoy. Did you know citrus fruit has many natural cancer fighting substances? The food factors in whole fruit are synergistic, which means because of the cooperation of the food factors, the total effect is greater than the sum of the effects when taken independently. And you thought they just tasted good! These muffins are a "healthy acid" food, so use moderation.

20 MINUTES TO PREPARE

25 - 30 MINUTES TO BAKE

OVEN TEMPERATURE 350°

MUFFIN TINS, LIGHTLY FLOUR

8 REGULAR OR 24 MINI MUFFINS

VARIATIONS

- Replace 1/2 cup spelt flour with 1/2 cup spelt flakes or use kamut.
- Replace spelt with gluten-free rice (see conversions on page 185).
- Add 1/2 cup coconut flakes and/or 1/2 cup chopped dates.
- Once baked, brush tops with honey and sprinkle with date sugar.
- Roll dough into 2" balls place onto well greased cookie sheet. Flatten, brush tops with honey and sprinkle with date sugar. Bake ten minutes for chewy cookies.
- Add 1 teaspoon cinnamon
- _____
- _____

Ingredients

- 3/4 cups pure Water
- 3 tablespoons ground Flax seeds

- 1 cup Date sugar
- 1 cup fresh squeezed Orange juice
- 1/2 cup Canola oil
- Zest from one small organic Orange

- 2 cups whole Spelt flour
  (non-hybrid wheat)
- 1/2 teaspoon Baking Soda
- 1/2 teaspoon Vitamin C Crystals
- 1/2 teaspoon Sea Salt

- 3/4 cup chopped Walnuts or Pecans (Optional)

PREPARATION

Soak flax seed with water for five minutes, combine with liquid ingredients. Add to the dry mix, stir till evenly moist. Stir in walnuts or pecans. The batter should be very thick. Gently press into well greased and floured muffin pan. Bake at 350° for 25 - 30 minutes.

SERVING SUGGESTIONS

Instead of muffins make a cake in a bunt pan and serve as part of an elegant brunch.

This is a special occasion treat. Too many of these will keep you acid. Keep this in the healthier acid-forming category.

Great to serve company! Wonderful side to Breakfast Salad, page 48.

* Note: This recipe is not recommended for a strict candida diet.

**Note: If using a non-alcohol vanilla increase amount to 1 tablespoon.

Very Berry Coffee Cake

Every now and then we all need a sweet treat. You don't need coffee to enjoy this one. If you are sensitive to berries, don't let that stop you, use another fruit. Even the harshest critic (and we all know one) will like this recipe.

The next time someone asks, what do you eat? You can say – cake!

20 MINUTES TO PREPARE

25 – 30 MINUTES TO BAKE

OVEN TEMPERATURE 350°

COOKIE SHEET OR PIZZA STONE

EIGHT SERVINGS

VARIATIONS

- Make cookies by rolling a 2" ball of dough in crushed nuts, flatten and indent center with thumb and place one piece of fruit in center. Cut ten minutes off of baking time. Makes 20 cookies.
- Make cookies omitting nuts and fruit, or just fruit.
- Instead of oblong, try round or square or heart shaped. Use dough to make a pie crust, bake and fill with fresh fruit.
- Decorate with various fruits. When hot out of the oven drizzle with maple syrup.

- _____

- _____

Ingredients

- 1 cup Quinoa flour · GLUTEN-FREE
- 1/4 cup Tapioca flour
- 1/4 teaspoon Sea Salt
- 1/2 teaspoon Baking Soda
- 1/2 teaspoon Vitamin C Crystals

- 3/4 cup chopped Pistachios or Quinoa Flakes
- 1 to 1-1/2 cup fresh frozen Raspberries

- 1/3 cup Sunflower oil
- 1 tablespoon Maple Syrup
- 1/4 teaspoon liquid Stevia
- 3 tablespoons pure Water
- 1 teaspoon Vanilla

PREPARATION

Combine first five dry ingredients in mixing bowl. Combine next five liquid ingredients and pour into dry, mixing with a spoon as you pour. Form into a large ball and refrigerate 15 minutes or overnight or freeze until needed.

Roll ball in chopped nuts or quinoa flakes. Place on a cookie sheet, flatten dough and form into a rectangle approximately 9" x 5". More nuts or flakes may need to be added to edges and bottom, make sure it is well coated.

Form a well in center with a one inch edge. Arrange frozen fruit in center (if fruit is not frozen it will dry out when baked). Bake at 350° for 25 - 30 minutes. Do not over cook.

SERVING SUGGESTIONS

When serving cut down center lengthwise, then cut across in two inch slices. If you do not plan to serve this right away or if you have leftovers or have made cookies, never stack pieces before freezing because they bond together.

Yes, this is poor food combining, but way better for you than a cheese danish. Remember the rule — cheat healthy!

 * Note: Maple syrup is still sugar be careful if on a candida diet.

** Note: If using a non-alcohol vanilla increase amount to 1 tablespoon.

Green Smoothie

Breakfast is just that; a break from the night's fast. What we eat or don't eat when we wake up will set the tone for the day. If we start with an acid meal, grab fast food for lunch and eat a high protein poorly combined meal for dinner, an acid pH will never have a chance to become balanced.

If you are like most of us, you are in a rush to get out the door. This Smoothie is a healthy meal you can fix fast and take with you to drink in the car.

5 MINUTES TO PREPARE

SHARP KNIFE &
CUTTING BOARD

BLENDER OR VITA MIX

VARIATIONS

- You may add any vegetable you wish, for example: broccoli, cilantro, substitute a lime in place of the lemon. Add cucumber, celery and parsley or anything you can think of.

- Replace spinach with a teaspoon of Stevia Plus powder and add 1 cup coconut milk for one cup of the water for a thicker "sweet" smoothie (omit the salt).

- This is a great way to add supplementation into your diet. Add whole food supplements such as Juice Plus™, or VidaCell™, or Heavenly Greens™, Udo's Choice Oil™ or acidophilus, etc.

Ingredients

- 1 ripe avocado, pitted and scooped out of the skin
- 1 whole lemon peeled
- 1 cup fresh organic spinach
- 1 tablespoon of powdered organic Wheat, Barley, and/or Kamut grass
- 16 ounces water from a pure source
- 3 or 4 ice cubes
- Sea Salt or Bragg Liquid Aminos to taste

PREPARATION

Place all ingredients into a blender or Vita Mix and blend on high until creamy. Adjust flavors and enjoy. The avocado is a powerhouse of nutrition and the "good" fat in the fruit will help neutralize the excess acid in your system.

Remember, how we start our morning will set the tone for the day that follows. If we start with coffee, bagel and cream cheese or bacon and eggs we are setting the stage for aches and pains, heartburn and a real slump mid afternoon.

SERVING SUGGESTIONS

Fast, easy and alkalizing. Best way I know to start the day or as a quick mid day pick-me-up.

Breakfast Salad

At first eating a salad for breakfast seems very strange. But, I guarantee you will learn to love it. I chop enough salad mix to last three or four days, then all I have to do is open the refrigerator and voile — breakfast, lunch or dinner is served. I can add avocado or olives or nuts or seeds to customize the basic mix or eat as is. I also make enough salad dressing to last the same length of time. Trust me, you will learn to crave this.

20 Minutes to Prepare
Cutting Board
Sharp Knife
Glass Storage Bowl with Cover
Glass Jar with Lid for Dressing
Servings Vary

VARIATIONS

- Be creative this is really a "kitchen-sink" recipe, throw it all in.
- Chop fine or tear into larger pieces. Use a food processor to shred, however, the larger the pieces the longer it will keep. Too busy to chop, buy precut fixin's at a natural market salad bar.
- Add cold steamed asparagus, artichoke hearts (sans vinegar), avocado (my favorite), green onions, ripe olives, sunflower seeds, almonds . . .

- _____

- _____

- _____

Ingredients

- 1 bag organic Spring Green Salad mix
- 1 large head organic Romaine lettuce
- 3 Carrots chopped or shredded
- 2 stalks Celery sliced thin
- 1 cup chopped or shredded Red Cabbage
- 1 Cucumber chopped
- 1 stalk Broccoli florettes

DRESSING

- 1/2 cup extra virgin Olive Oil
- 2 organic Lemons juiced
- 1 teaspoon non-irradiated dried or fresh herb such as Basil
- 3 drops liquid Stevia
- Sea Salt to taste

PREPARATION

Wash and clean the vegetables. Chop to desired size and mix together. Add desired variations. Add ingredients such as avocado to individual salad as needed. Avocados do not store well and will turn brown once cut. Refrigerate unused portion.

Mix dressing ingredients in a jar with a lid. Add dressing to individual servings as needed and enjoy. Refrigerate unused portion.

SERVING SUGGESTIONS

Bring to the office for lunch. Serve as a quick side for dinner. Top with cold left over brown rice or quinoa or beans.

What Are the Basics for Wellness?

- Good clean well oxygenated air where we sleep at night and in our homes.
- Drink a minimum of half your body weight in ounces of pure source high pH water everyday, never drink tap water. If you drink distilled add a good trace mineral or fresh lemon juice.
- Eat organic foods low on the food chain such as: green high vibrational, high pH forming vegetables. Eliminate all processed foods.
- Walk 3,000 steps (about 40 minutes) outside everyday in one outing.
- Allow the sun to shine on your face before noon everyday, outside without glasses or sunscreen. This can be done during your walk.
- Do a deep breathing meditation 20 minutes everyday for maintenance. Increase to 20 minutes twice a day for healing. This can also be done during your walk.
- Get a minimum of 35-40 grams of fiber everyday - read labels, you will be shocked at how little fiber you get everyday.
- Take in plenty of essential fatty acids (flax seeds or oil, evening primrose oil, borage oil, fish oil), our body does not produce these and they are essential for cellular communication.
- Make sure you are getting plenty of enzymes in live foods or if need be, supplement.
- Eliminate all man made chemicals in your living space both inside, on, in and around your body.
- Replace feather, foam and polyester pillows, comforters and mattress covers with 100% cotton along with all bedding materials.
- Read all labels, if it can not be found in nature don't buy it.
- Protect yourself from electromagnetic fields.
- Turn off the TV and spend time with your family, read, play board games or start a hobby.
- Finally, and most importantly, clear your mind of toxic thoughts. Forgiveness is the most selfish act we can do. Find beauty and acknowledge it throughout your day. Something as simple as a fresh flower on your desk can connect us with all the beauty of the world. ∎

Yeast Free & Alternative Grain Breads

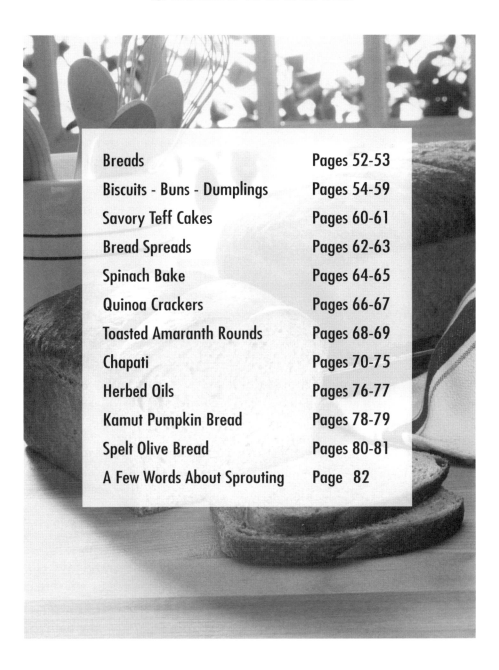

Breads

Is the staff of life beating you over the head? Next to sugar, wheat is the most eaten food in this country. In places where rice is the staple, many people are allergic to rice, but in this country it's wheat. Gluten sensitivities are among the most misdiagnosed health concerns in the nation. Sensitivities and allergies are insidious things - especially if you are eating the same foods every day and at every meal, as is true of wheat. Then to make

matters worse, it's refined and bleached and yeast is added along with sugar, dairy, eggs and chemical ingredients. See what I mean? Before long we have chronic gas, diarrhea, constipation or other stomach disorders, or we have a headache, chronic cold, urinary tract disorders or skin problems. After a while we accept these things as a way of life. Trust me, they shouldn't be!

Wheat may need to be avoided for several reasons - one might be an allergy to the wheat itself. Wheat also contains a chemical which, when consumed by some people, causes depression.

For others, the culprit is the gluten. Perhaps you just wish to broaden your horizons and rotate grains. Remember, variety, moderation and consistency is an important part of a healthy lifestyle.

NOTE: Spelt and Kamut are non-hybrid forms of wheat. Spelt also contains more gluten than wheat. Depending on the reason you are avoiding wheat, please be careful and consult a health care professional. Some people can eat Spelt but not Wheat or Kamut! The only common non-gluten grains are corn and rice. Wheat is a member of the Grass Family (white flour is wheat). Other members of the Grass Family are oats, rye, millet, rice and corn - see the Food Family Section, pages 10-17. So don't make the mistake so many people make, including myself in the beginning, eating rice one day, and rye (the main ingredient in rye bread is wheat) the next, and oats the next, barley, etc. Even if you don't rotate foods I encourage you to try amaranth, quinoa and teff, all delicious and densely nutritious.

Avoiding wheat is especially difficult if you are on the road all the time or on a vacation. How many times have you gone on vacation and come home sick? Could it be the food you have been eating? The best advice I can give you is never eat anything you know is going to make you sick. For example, if you have no choice and have to eat in a fast food restaurant, be smart. Order a salad, no cheese or croutons, with a lemon wedge for dressing and a broiled chicken breast, then THROW AWAY THE BUN. Even if eating chicken and a salad is not the correct rotational thing to do, I would much rather see you do that than scarf a bacon cheese burger with fries and a cola! If you are a vegetarian, order two salads and skip the chicken.

Monday and Thursday I make a large salad mix base to use through the week. You can buy this pre made at most natural markets and grocery stores. This salad has become my "fast-food". Learn to go after what you want instead of accepting what is handed to you.

Be street smart and learn which restaurant can accommodate you best. Order rice in place of pasta, or double-up on the vegetable. If you know you have a rough week ahead, bake on Saturday and make and freeze daily care packages. For vacations, I have had food sent on ahead packed in dry ice. My carry on luggage is filled with frozen food and ice packs. For driving trips, a cooler in the trunk of the car works well too. Think like a pioneer, because that is what you are!

Biscuits-Buns-Dumplings

As you may have already guessed, a simple recipe can go a long way. Just as the climb up to a mountain top changes with the starting point, so it is with food. I experimented with a lot of recipes before I hit on this one. Experiment for yourself, create a dish I haven't even thought of. Also, try the Spelt Olive Bread on page 80. It is a perfect example of a variation being as good as the original recipe.

10 MINUTES TO PREPARE

20 - 25 MINUTES TO BAKE

COOKIE SHEET, BAKING STONE

SAUCE PAN, BOWL, SPOON

OVEN TEMPERATURE 375°

6 - 8 BISCUITS

VARIATIONS

- Roll thin and bake on a cookie sheet. While still warm cut into cracker size pieces. To crisp up return to a 200° oven for another 10 to 15 minutes.
- Play with shapes. Use cookie cutters for fun shapes or cut out a shape the size of a slice of bread.
- Double or triple recipe and bake in a bread pan for 45 minutes. If you do this, use oiled wax paper on bottom and oil and flour the entire pan as well. This method does not work with amaranth.
- Add vegetables, nuts, seeds or herbs.
- _____
- _____

Ingredients

QUINOA - GLUTEN-FREE

- 1 cup pure Water
- 1/3 cup ground Flax seeds
- 1 tablespoon Sunflower oil
- 1 cup Quinoa flour
- 1/2 cup Tapioca flour or ground Sunflower seeds
- 1 teaspoon Baking Soda
- 1/2 teaspoon Vitamin C Crystals
- 1/2 teaspoon Sea Salt (optional)
- 1 tablespoon Quinoa flour
- 1 tablespoon Sunflower oil

OAT or BARLEY - GLUTEN

- 1 cup pure Water
- 1 teaspoon Agar Agar flakes
- 1 tablespoon Sesame oil
- 1 cup Oat or Barley flour
- 1/2 cup whole Rolled Oats or Barley Flakes
- 1 teaspoon Baking Soda
- 1/2 teaspoon Vitamin C Crystals
- 1/2 teaspoon Sea Salt (optional)
- 1 tablespoon Oat or Barley flour
- 1 tablespoon Sesame oil

Ingredients

RICE - GLUTEN-FREE

- 1 cup pure Water or Rice beverage
- 1 tablespoon Agar Agar flakes
- 1 teaspoon Vanilla (optional)***
- 1 tablespoon Sesame or Almond oil**
- 1-1/2 cups Rice flour
- 1 teaspoon Baking Soda
- 1/2 teaspoon Vitamin C Crystals
- 1/2 teaspoon Sea Salt (optional)

- 1 tablespoon Rice flour or Sesame seeds*
- 1 tablespoon Sesame or Almond oil** *

SPELT OR KAMUT - NON-HYBRID WHEAT

- 1 cup pure Water
- 1 tablespoon Agar Agar flakes
- 1 tablespoon light Olive oil
- 1-1/2 cups Spelt or Kamut flour
- 1 teaspoon Baking Soda
- 1/2 teaspoon Vitamin C Crystals
- 1/2 teaspoon Sea Salt
  (optional)

- 1 tablespoon Spelt or
  Kamut flour
- 1 tablespoon light
  Olive oil

Note: Use these ingredients to oil and flour baking sheet.
**Note: Use different oil if allergic to almonds.*
***Note: If using a non-alcohol vanilla, please increase amount to 1 tablespoon.*

Ingredients

AMARANTH - GLUTEN-FREE

- 1 cup pure Water
- 1/3 cup ground Flax seeds
- 1 tablespoon Canola oil
- 3/4 cup Amaranth flour
- 1/4 cup finely ground Hazel Nuts (optional)
- 1/2 cup Arrowroot starch
- 1 teaspoon Baking Soda
- 1/2 teaspoon Vitamin C Crystals
- 1/2 teaspoon Sea Salt (optional)

- 1 tablespoon Amaranth flour*
- 1 tablespoon Canola oil*

TEFF - GLUTEN-FREE

- 1 cup pure Water
- 1 tablespoon Agar Agar flakes
- 1 tablespoon Walnut oil or olive oil
- 1 cup Teff flour
- 1/2 cup ground Walnuts or Pecans or Carob
- 1 teaspoon Baking Soda
- 1/2 teaspoon Vitamin C Crystals
- 1/2 teaspoon Sea Salt (optional)

- 1 tablespoon Teff flour*
- 1 tablespoon Walnut oil or olive oil*

Note: Use these ingredients to oil and flour baking sheet.

Place water and ground flax seeds or agar agar, in a bowl, soak for 15 minutes. Add oil and any variation at this time.

In a separate bowl combine all of the dry ingredients.

Add the mixed liquid to the mixed dry ingredients and combine with a spoon. Turn out onto a lightly floured surface and knead a minute or so. If too sticky to knead make drop biscuits, adding more flour will make the biscuits tough. With the palm of your hand flatten to about a 1/2 inch thickness. Using a glass, cookie cutter or knife cut into desired shapes. Knead scraps and continue to cut until it is all used. If you happen to have a baking stone this would be a good time to use it. However, a non-reactive oiled and floured cake pan or cookie sheet will also work. If you wish, you may make drop biscuits.

Place in a preheated 375° oven for 20 to 25 minutes. Once baked, tops may be brushed with Herbed Oils, pages 76-77.

A nice addition to breakfast, lunch, dinner or a snack any time. May be frozen before or after baking. Leftovers may be broken into crumbs and used as a stuffing or topping to add interest and nutrition to another meal. Slice baked biscuit into 1/4 inch slices lengthwise and toast in a 250° oven for 10 to 15 minutes, use as you would bagel or pita chips.

Place dollops of dough on top of a casserole and bake till brown on top. Knead and roll flat, cut a star out of center and use as top crust of a pot pie.

Excellent as a yeast free 'bread' for sandwiches. Very good with Breakfast Salad pages 48-49.

Savory Teff Cakes

Teff has been an Ethiopian staple for thousands of years. It is the smallest of all the grains, but don't let its size fool you, the taste is gigantic. These pan breads are so good when served with a side of asparagus or snow peas. In minutes you will have a complete and hearty meal. The first time I tried this recipe I couldn't stop eating. I guarantee when you realize how quick and easy these are to make and how wonderful they taste, you will make them often.

20 MINUTES TO PREPARE

4 MINUTES PER CAKE (COOK 3 AT A TIME)

HEAVY SKILLET OR GRIDDLE, STOVE TOP

BOWL, SPOON, KNIFE, CUTTING BOARD

TWELVE 4" BREADS

VARIATIONS

- Spoon batter into a well oiled, oven safe baking dish approximately 8" square or 9" round. Place into a 350° pre heated oven for 50 minutes or until it tests done in center. Cut into squares or wedges and serve as you would corn bread.

- Double amount of nuts, olives and onion. Drop heaping teaspoons of batter onto greased cookie sheet and bake in a 375° oven for 20 minutes and serve as hors d'oeuvre or half time munchies.

- Substitute different veggies and or herbs.

- _____

- _____

- _____

Ingredients

- 2 cups Teff flour
- 1/2 teaspoon Sea Salt
- 1 teaspoon Baking Soda
- 1/2 teaspoon Vitamin C Crystals
- 3 tablespoons Ex. V. Olive oil plus enough for griddle
- 1-1/2 cups Bay Leaf tea. To make tea boil 2 cups water and 3 whole Bay Leaves (broken) for 5 minutes, allow to steep another 10, remove Bay Leaves, (this tea was my grandmother Calabria's remedy for an upset stomach)
- 3 tablespoons each fresh minced Onion, chopped Green Olives and chopped Walnuts or Pine Nuts (omit nuts if allergic).
- Serve with roasted Garlic paste, Variations page 94

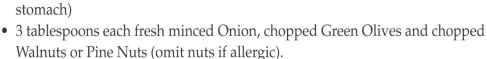

PREPARATION

Preheat pan or griddle on medium high.

Combine first five ingredients. Make a well in center and add half of the bay leaf water. Add oil and start to mix, bringing more flour into center. Add remaining water and combine well. Batter should be thick. Add remaining ingredients.

Add olive oil to pan and drop batter by spoonfuls until approximately 4" in diameter. Brown on bottom and flip, press down with spatula and brown other side. Continue until all batter is gone.

SERVING SUGGESTIONS

Serve as a savory bread to accompany a "green" meal or as a quick snack or appetizer.

Bread Spreads

Butter may be the last dairy hold out. Ice Cream and cheese was tough, but sweet creamery butter? No one ever said this was going to be easy. Look for different tastes - savory or crunchy. Remember nothing is going to taste like butter, so enjoy the alternatives with an open mind and don't compare. Enjoy different things for their own merits. There is so much wrong with margarine, please do not use that as a butter substitute. Try Ghee (a clarified butter which is casein and lactose free), it may be the only dairy your body can tolerate.

TIMES WILL VARY

UTENSILS WILL VARY

METHODS WILL VARY

AMOUNTS WILL VARY

IDEAS

- Sunflower Butter or as the 'meat' in a sandwich - mix in raw hulled sunflower seeds and serve with lettuce and thinly sliced cooked beet slices.
- A sandwich I enjoy is sesame tahini, avocado slices and alfalfa sprouts on yeast free spelt or brown rice bread or a Biscuit, pages 54-59. Try brown rice mochi toasted crisp in a waffle iron, eat open face. Top with mashed avocado.
- Cashew butter or almond butter or pistachio butter.
- Herbed Oils pages 76-77.
- These spreads are a great place to add minced sea vegetables or wheat grass for extra nutrition.
- _____
- _____

Ingredients

HUMMUS HEALTHY ACID FORMING

- 2 cups cooked Chic Peas mashed to a paste - or - 1 cup toasted Garbanzo flour and 1-1/2 cups pure Water cooked together until smooth and thick
- 4 tablespoons Lemon juice
- 4 tablespoons Sesame Tahini
- 2 tablespoons extra virgin Olive oil
- 1 clove Garlic finely minced (optional)
- 1/2 teaspoon Sea Salt or to taste

PREPARATION

Using a spoon blend all ingredients together or blend until smooth and creamy in a food processor. You may adjust the consistency with additional water one tablespoon at a time.

PUMPKIN SEED PEST ALKALIZING

- 1-1/2 cups raw shelled Pumpkin Seeds (cover with pure water and soak 8 hours)
- 1 cup fresh Basil or herb of choice
- 1/4 cup extra virgin Olive Oil
- 2 cloves garlic minced (optional)
- Sea salt to taste

PREPARATION

Drain pumpkin seeds, reserve water. Place seeds and all remaining ingredients (except water) in a food processor and process until smooth. Add reserved water as needed to achieve creamy texture. Excellent on rice crackers or tossed with buckwheat soba or rice pasta.

Spinach Bake

This is an unusual pan bread. Cut into slender wedges it's an excellent finger food that transports well. This recipe is a perfect example of the many uses for the pancake and waffle batters. Not unlike the egg frittata my mother always made. This version uses no eggs and is good cold. Make a 'Pizza Crust' variation, just bake in a 9 x 13" cake or round pizza pan and top with fresh chopped basil, onions or any fresh topping you like.

10 Minutes to Prepare
Bake 35 - 45 Minutes
Mixing Bowl, Spoon
9" Round Oven Safe Baking Dish
350° Oven
Serves 4 as Side Dish - 2 as Main Dish

VARIATIONS

- Substitute swiss chard, dandelion, kale or mustard greens for the spinach.
- Use batter made from another flour, see pages 32-35.
- Any fresh chopped vegetable will work or try a different fresh herb or spice.

- _____

- _____

Ingredients

- 1 bunch fresh organic Spinach, washed and minced

- 1 recipe Quinoa Pancake batter, Page 33

- Oil and Quinoa Flour for bottom of pan

PREPARATION

Wash spinach, being sure to get all of the grit off of the leaves. Remove stems and discard. Chop leaves into small pieces.

Prepare Quinoa Pancake/Waffle batter according to directions. Fold in the spinach until all is evenly coated. Turn out into an oiled and floured 9" round baking dish.

Bake 35 to 45 minutes in a 350° oven or until center tests dry.

SERVING SUGGESTIONS

Serve as a savory bread to accompany a "green" meal or as a quick snack or appetizer.

Quinoa Crackers

I was shocked when I read the label on a box of crackers to find yeast as an ingredient. How could this be, they are so flat! Quinoa Crackers are so hearty and good you will never miss your old crackers! Crumbs can be made from any of the bread substitutes in this book, however, the crumbs from this recipe are my favorite. All the seasonings you need are already in the crackers.

20 Minutes to Prepare
40-45 Minutes to Bake
Cookie Sheet & Rolling Pin
Oven Temperature 300°
19 Dozen 1-1/2" Crackers

VARIATIONS

- Add sesame seeds or ground nuts.
- Increase tapioca by 1/2 cup and roll dough into 1/2" by 8" ropes and twist into pretzels, bake until golden.
- If you know your only purpose for the crackers will be crumbs, crumble dough directly onto cookie sheet and bake as is.
- Slice into sticks and fry in a little coconut oil, salt and satisfy a junk food craving.
- _____
- _____
- _____

Ingredients

- 2 cups Quinoa flour
- 1/2 cup Tapioca flour
- 1 cup ground hulled Sunflower seeds
- 1 teaspoon Baking Soda
- 1/2 teaspoon Vitamin C Crystals
- 1/2 teaspoon Sea Salt (optional)

- 1-1/2 cups pure Water
- 1/4 cup Flax seeds ground
- 1/2 cup Sunflower oil

PREPARATION

Soak ground flax seeds in water and oil for 15 minutes.

While flax seeds are soaking place all dry ingredients in a processor or bowl and blend well. Add liquid ingredients and mix by hand or until ball forms in processor. If too dry add more water one tablespoon at a time, if too sticky do the same with the flour. Divide into 3 equal balls. If you do not wish to bake three trays of crackers now the dough may be frozen and used another day, (do not thaw in microwave).

Using your hands, press dough as evenly as possible in an oiled and floured cookie sheet (a baking stone works best). The dough will be sticky, however, using a wet rolling pin should help, roll dough flat and cut into 1-1/2" squares or desired size. Bake in a 300° oven for 40 - 45 minutes or until golden. Allow to cool for 5 minutes, then using a spatula loosen and enjoy.

SERVING SUGGESTIONS

Enjoy as is or make into crumbs to add flavor to veggies or fish.

Toasted Amaranth Rounds

Are you missing the crunch of a really good cracker? Do you long for something to munch along with your carrot sticks? Don't despair. These are wonderful! The batter is a snap to make, but because of the double baking, allow enough time.

Amaranth (also known as Kiwicha) originated with the Aztec. It is a complete vegetable-grain protein containing the amino acid lysine, and is an excellent choice if on a vegetarian diet.

5 MINUTES TO PREPARE
60 MINUTES TOTAL TO BAKE
MIXING BOWL, SPOON, COOKIE SHEET
375° & 300° OVEN
6 DOZEN 2" CRACKERS

VARIATIONS

- Do not cut in half to re-bake for crackers, leave in biscuit form and make great mini sandwiches, fill with thinly sliced cucumber and watercress.
- Leftover crackers are great made into crumbs, freeze and toss with veggies another day.
- Add poppy seeds, sesame seeds or nigella seeds, replace 1/2 cup of amaranth with 1/2 cup finely ground hazelnuts.
- See Veggie Pot Pie pages 128-129.
- _____
- _____
- _____

Ingredients

- 2 cups + 2 tablespoons Amaranth flour, separated
- 1/2 teaspoon each Baking Soda -
  Vitamin C Crystals -
  Sea Salt

- 1-1/2 cup warm pure Water
- 3 tablespoons Canola oil

PREPARATION

Using a spoon, mix all dry ingredients, minus the 2 tablespoons amaranth. Mix together warm water and canola oil, add to dry ingredients and mix just till evenly moistened.

Lightly oil cookie sheet and sprinkle with 1 tablespoon reserved amaranth flour per batch. Using a teaspoon drop batter onto the prepared cookie sheet. Once cooked the centers will be more like a thick pudding rather than bread - it is for that reason I suggest you keep the diameter of each biscuit no more 2 inches across. Bake in a 375° oven for 30 minute. The outside should be golden, remove from oven and allow to cool. When all batches are done, turn oven down to 300°, remove biscuits from cookie sheet When cool enough to handle, use a sharp knife cut in half lengthwise to produce two rounds. Place cut side down on cookie sheet and return to oven and bake at 300° for another 20 - 30 minutes or until crisp. Freeze any extras.

SERVING SUGGESTIONS

This is a great snack food. A crunchy munchy other than a carrot stick - not that I have anything against a carrot stick, just that sometimes we do not live by carrot sticks alone.

Chapati

T here are dozens of uses for these wonderful little flat breads, they are a staple of East Indian cuisine and once you have tried them you will know why. The ingredients are basic and almost all of the grain alternatives will work. Since conversions can be tricky I will give a recipe for each one. Also, traditionally these breads are brushed with ghee. Ghee is clarified butter and is casein and lactose free, look for it in your local health food store. As an alternative may I suggest Herbed Oils, see pages 76-77.

12 FLAT BREADS 6" TO 7" ACROSS

A HEAVY SKILLET WORKS BEST

15 MINUTES TO PREPARE BY HAND METHOD

5 MINUTES TO PREPARE WITH FOOD PROCESSOR

A COUPLE OF MINUTES PER BREAD TO COOK

VARIATIONS

- For quinoa flour, substitute 1/2 cup ground raw shelled sunflower seed, flax seed, pistachio, cashew or macadamia nuts for 1/2 cup of flour. Perhaps instead of mixing these into the bread mix, flatten dough into the seeds or nuts before cooking.

- Of the grass family, rice flour and oat flour have the best taste on their own, but can be mixed half and half with barley, millet, rye or each other. One half cup ground almonds or whole sesame seeds work well with the rice or oat flours. A tablespoon of anise, dill, fennel or nigella seeds are nice in the rye mix. Breads made with these flours are the most dry and crumble easily, however they taste great.

- _____

- _____

Variations

- Amaranth flour and poppy seeds are a great team, two tablespoons seeds mixed into the dough or placed on the counter top to flatten the prepared dough into, either way it's good!
- Spelt and kamut make the chewiest and most tender Chapati. If you like, either one can be cut half and half with teff flour. A teaspoon of either basil, sage, thyme, oregano, savory, marjoram or rosemary is nice to add to the dough.
- Chick Pea flour makes a crisp cracker-like disc and can be used as a corn tortilla substitute. Allow to air dry and reheat and crisp in oven.
- The dough makes a great calzone to fill with your own creation or pizza crust, if not divided. Pasties or pot pie crust or tortilla. . . only your imagination will limit you, see Lunch Pockets pages 126-127.
- The oat bread makes a great shortbread.
- Sandwiches may be rolled, folded or stacked. Try a double decker "club" cut into quarters for easy handling.
- Cut into sixth's, place in a single layer on a cookie sheet and bake in a 300° oven till crisp, about 10 minutes, time will vary with the grain used. You now have easy (and tasty) crackers. Crush the crackers and you have crumbs to sprinkle on vegetables, salad or use for a stuffing.
- The best variations are the ones you think of.
- Before you try any of these variations, please, make Chapati plain and enjoy the simple pleasures of the basics.

- _____

- _____

- _____

- _____

- _____

Ingredients

QUINOA GLUTEN-FREE

- 1-1/2 cups Quinoa flour
- 1/2 cup Tapioca flour
- 2 tablespoons Sunflower oil
- 1/2 cup pure Water

FAVORITE VARIATION

- _____
- _____
- _____
- _____

OAT GLUTEN

- 2-1/4 cups Oat flour
- 2 tablespoons Almond oil
- 1/2 cup pure Water

FAVORITE VARIATION

- _____
- _____
- _____

RICE GLUTEN-FREE

- 2-1/4 cups Rice flour
- 2 tablespoons Sesame oil
- 1/2 cup pure Water

FAVORITE VARIATION

- _____
- _____
- _____

AMARANTH GLUTEN-FREE FAVORITE VARIATION

- 1-1/2 cups Amaranth flour
- 1/2 cup Arrowroot starch
- 2 tablespoons Canola oil
- 1/2 cup pure Water

- _____
- _____
- _____
- _____

Ingredients

SPELT NON-HYBRID WHEAT

- 2 cups Spelt flour
- 2 tablespoons Safflower oil
- 1/2 cup pure Water

FAVORITE VARIATION

- _____
- _____
- _____

KAMUT NON-HYBRID WHEAT

- 2 cups Kamut flour
- 2 tablespoons light Olive oil
- 1/2 cup pure Water

FAVORITE VARIATION

- _____
- _____
- _____

TEFF GLUTEN-FREE

- 2-1/4 cups Teff flour
- 2 tablespoons Safflower oil
- 1/2 cup pure Water

FAVORITE VARIATION

- _____
- _____
- _____

CHICK PEA FLOUR
GLUTEN-FREE

- 2-1/2 cups Chick Pea flour
- 2 tablespoons ex.v. Olive oil
- 1 tablespoon Lime juice
- 1/2 cup pure Water
- 1 teaspoon cumin

FAVORITE VARIATION

- _____
- _____
- _____
- _____
- _____

Preparation

FOOD PROCESSOR METHOD

Place all dry ingredients into the bowl of a food processor. Reserve enough flour for your countertop, each Chapati will stick when rolled flat without a 'dusting' of flour on the work surface. Close lid to processor and process, while running, add oil through hole on top. If necessary stop machine and scrape sides, to insure even distribution of oil. With processor running, slowly add water. A ball of dough should form. If not, continue to add extra water 1 tablespoon at a time until it holds together and no longer crumbles. Once again, if necessary, stop machine and scrape sides. A ball should form and whir around in the bowl of the processor. Stop machine and remove dough onto a floured surface and kneed a couple of minutes.*

HAND METHOD

In a bowl mix all dry ingredients. Add oil and cut in until evenly distributed. Make a well in center and add water, stir. With your hands, work dough until soft and elastic. If it continues to crumble add more water one tablespoonful at a time until it holds together and forms a soft elastic ball. Turn out onto a lightly floured surface and knead 5 to 10 minutes.*

*At this point directions are the same for Food Processor & Hand Method.

Preparation

SHAPING CHAPATI

Roll into a 12" rope, cover with a damp cloth and allow to rest ten minutes.

In the mean time, heat a heavy skillet or griddle. Select prepared oil to baste the finished bread Herbed Oils pages 76-77 or use Ghee. This step is not necessary if you want the bread to be crisp for use as a tostada, etc. A covered, oven proof glass bowl is also helpful to keep the bread tender and warm. As a general rule these should be eaten immediately. The dough could be prepared in advance if wrapped in a damp cloth and kept in the refrigerator for a day, or frozen for up to a week and thawed the day you plan its use. This is also a good time to prepare any ground nuts or seeds you may wish to flatten into the dough.

Unwrap your dough and cut into 1" pieces. Form each section into a ball and flatten with your hands, keeping as round as possible. Place on a flat, lightly floured surface, using a rolling pin, roll until about 5" to 7" across. I like to cook as I go, but you may prefer to complete this step first. Be sure to keep the dough covered with a sheet of unbleached wax paper in between as you stack so they will not bond together or dry out at this stage.

Place each disc on the dry heated heavy skillet or griddle, adjust heat so as not to burn the chapati, no oil or flour is necessary. If the dough begins to bubble up press down with a spatula. Flip the chapati over when pale brown spots begin to form on the bottom. Do the same on the other side and for all remaining breads. Brush each one with oil before stacking in covered dish. To keep warm place dish into an 150° oven until time to serve.

See Variations for leftover suggestions or freeze for another use.

SERVING SUGGESTIONS

Limitless. At home or on the road these are easy to transport and even easier for you to enjoy.

Herbed Oils

Expeller pressed oil is a healthy alternative to butter. A large variety of ready made oils have become available in most specialty stores. Italian restaurants also have begun to place olive oil with a garlic clove and herbs in the bottle, at tables for 'dipping'. Another alternative might be nut oils, hazel nut is quite yummy! Be sure to purchase only cold pressed or expeller pressed oils to insure no solvents or chemicals were used to extract the oil. Baked, sauteed or straight-up, oils are a tasty and healthy solution to butter or margarine.

15 MINUTES PLUS 4 TO 8 HOURS TO INFUSE

SMALL SAUCE PAN

QUART JAR/BOTTLE WITH CORK OR LID

2 CUPS OIL

VARIATIONS

- I am going to give one recipe. . . anything goes. You may substitute any of the following: sunflower oil and tarragon, sesame oil and dill, canola oil and mustard seed, walnut oil and citron, etc.
- Use non-irradiated dried herbs, one teaspoon should equal one large sprig of fresh herb.
- _____
- _____

Note: If allergic to tree nuts do not use oils such as walnut oil or hazelnut oil.

Ingredients

- 2 cups extra virgin Olive Oil, divided
- 4 large sprigs fresh Sweet Basil
- 1 clove Garlic peeled (optional)

PREPARATION

Use hot soapy water to thoroughly wash quart jar to be used, air dry jar. In cool water wash and dry basil. Peel garlic. Heat one cup oil, do not boil or allow to steam. If the oil is too hot for your finger it is over heated. Place basil and garlic into a jar pour in warm oil. Allow to infuse for 4 to 8 hours. Strain into a serving bottle. If you wish, the herbed oil may be placed in the original olive oil bottle or decorative bottle with a cork. Add remaining cup oil and enjoy.

SERVING SUGGESTIONS

Try a tablespoon of hazel nut oil in a bowl of cream of buckwheat cereal, add a few drops of stevia.

A natural for salads or sautes.

Use oils to add extra flavor to flat breads, chapati or pancakes.

Use in creamed soups.

Store in a cool, dark place. Refrigeration will cause some oils to solidify

Keep a winter window-sill herb garden. It looks great, is fun to play with and will save money at the grocers.

Kamut Pumpkin Bread

Even though kamut is a non-hybrid wheat, I find the flavor and texture to be more like corn. Whatever it may remind you of, you will agree it is delightful. When I first started my diversified rotary diet, kamut was not listed. Not knowing any better, I put it in with my day three rotation which was incorrect because wheat, kamut and spelt are too closely related to eat three days in a row. We enjoyed this bread so much I chose not to change it. Not sweet like traditional pumpkin bread, you may wish to serve it with vegetables rather than as a dessert.

15 MINUTES TO PREPARE

60 MINUTES TO BAKE

BREAD PAN, BOWL, SPOON

OVEN TEMPERATURE 350°

ONE LOAF OF BREAD

VARIATIONS

- This will also work with spelt flour.
- Replace pumpkin with another squash or sweet potato.
- Add a different nut, seed or chopped fruit.
- Make muffins instead of bread.
- If you can tolerate soy milk or rice milk use in place of water.
- _____
- _____

Ingredients

- 2 cups Kamut flour - NON-HYBRID WHEAT
- 1 teaspoon Baking Soda
- 1/2 teaspoon Vitamin C Crystals
- 1/2 teaspoon Sea Salt (optional)
- 2 teaspoons ground Cinnamon
- 1/4 teaspoon each ground Allspice, Cloves, Ginger
- 1/2 teaspoon powder Stevia
- 1/2 cup chopped Walnuts (optional)
- One 15oz. can Pumpkin or 2 cups fresh Pumpkin puree
- 1/3 cup Walnut Oil or Coconut Oil
- 1/2 cup pure Water
- Oil and Flour for bottom of pan

PREPARATION

In a large bowl combine all dry ingredients. In another bowl combine pumpkin, oil and water. Combine pumpkin mixture with dry ingredients, until all is evenly moist.

Oil bottom and sides of bread pan. Spoon batter evenly into bottom of pan, smooth top with spoon. Rub oil into top of batter and using a sharp knife make 1/4" deep slits in a diamond pattern on top of loaf. Bake in a 350° pre heated oven for 60 minutes. Allow to cool before slicing.

SERVING SUGGESTIONS

This is an excellent side with most meals. It transports well and is good to bring along when eating away from home. Healthy acid-forming, eat with plenty of fresh veggies for balance.

Spelt Olive Bread

I love this bread. It is easy to make and easy to eat. The best description would be dense and savory. Experiment, this is a variation from Biscuits - Buns - Dumplings, your variation may be better than anything I could think of. Serving this bread with a vegetable makes a hearty meal, although I have been known to make a meal of just the bread! Remember spelt is a non-hybrid wheat so use caution if you are avoiding wheat or gluten!

20 Minutes to Prepare

60-65 Minutes to Bake

Bowl, Spoon, Knife, Cutting Board

Oiled Wax Paper, Floured Bread Pan

Oven Temperature 350°

One Loaf of Bread

VARIATIONS

- Use nuts, seeds, chopped onion, cooked wild rice in place of olives.
- Experiment with a different grain, use another recipe from Biscuits - Buns - Dumplings pages 54-59. Unless mixed with another grain amaranth will not work.

- _____

- _____

- _____

- _____

Ingredients

- Double recipe Spelt Biscuits page 56. · NON-HYBRID WHEAT
  (2-1/2 cups total flour is recommended)

- 1 cup pitted and chopped oil packed
  Greek Olives

- Olive oil and extra flour for bottom of pan

PREPARATION

Follow batter directions for Spelt Biscuits be sure to double all ingredients. Once batter is made add olives or a variation and gently mix together.

Cut a piece of unbleached wax paper to fit into the bottom of the bread pan. Oil paper top and bottom, place into pan. Oil sides and lightly flour inside surface of bread pan. Gently pour batter into pan, smooth top and bake in a pre heated 350° oven for 60 to 65 minutes. It is done when a knife inserted in center comes out clean.

The longer it rests the easier it will stay together when sliced. I have also found that if frozen and thawed before slicing, it will stay in one piece better for an avocado, lettuce and cucumber sandwich. Remove wax paper before serving.

SERVING SUGGESTIONS

Wonderful "healthy acid-forming" addition to an all vegetable meal. Be sure to do proper food combining with this bread to avoid heart burn.

A Few Words
About Sprouting

I feel I need to say a few words about sprouting. The thought of sprouting seeds, beans and grains can seem obsessive, time consuming and hard to do. I know this because that is what I used to think. Sprouting does not need to be this big mysterious thing. Just the opposite, it is easy and takes less time than toasting a bagel. Sprouting will save money at the market. For pennies sprouted grains, seeds and beans deliver a big pay off. Because of the magic of sprouting, acid foods become an alkaline powerhouse of enzymes, vitamins, minerals and proteins. Once sprouted beans become a high pH food, beans no longer cause gas, bloat or heartburn, because they are more easily digested and assimilated they actually improve the efficiency of digestion.

Start small with a glass quart canning jar. Choose a bean that is easy to sprout and will sprout quickly such as mung beans. Buy a good quality fresh organic bean and sort to eliminate any broken or damaged beans (they will only rot). I use a piece of plastic screening material to cover the top, an old nylon or cheese cloth will work just as well. You can use a rubber band to hold the screen to the top of the jar, or the ring portion of a canning lid. Cover the bottom of the jar with beans. Fill the jar with filtered water (I use distilled) and allow to soak 24 hours. These will need a cool dark environment, I keep mine in a top cabinet next to my sink. Drain through the screening, rinse and put back into the cabinet. Repeat the rinsing and draining twice a day until the beans sprout, around three days. I use the soaking/rinsing water on my plants, it's better than fertilizer and the price is right. Once fully sprouted add to salads, soups and vegetable dishes. Refrigerate any unused portions.

The most important part of sprouting is the feeling of being connected with the cycle of life. After a while you will have several jars lined up with different beans and seeds waiting for you to enjoy. This is a fabulous activity to do with children. The energy these little powerhouses of nutrition will give you will make you wonder why it took you so long to sprout! ■

Soups & Vegetables

Soups & Vegetables

Vegetables natures gift to mankind. Eat them for breakfast, lunch and dinner - your grocery bills will plummet, your energy and stamina will increase ten fold, unwanted fat will melt away. What an ingenious way to fuel a machine. Eating should be (and was meant to be) a pleasure rather than a chore. Give me one good reason why a person can't eat a big bowl of steamed broccoli for lunch, or breakfast. It seems quite natural to me. Why does a meal need to be a big production every day?

As a culture we are so fortunate. We have the world at our fingertips, yet we choose to eat a cheese burrito and a diet drink for lunch. Instead of stopping for a jelly donut and coffee as an afternoon pick-me-up, stop at a place with a salad bar. Load your plate to the top with veggies. Whip out those Quinoa Crackers you put in your pocket before you left the house in anticipation of getting hungry. Instead of pretending hunger isn't going to happen, plan for and eat something that is going to make you feel good twice; first when you are eating it and again the next day.

A four star restaurant, in my opinion, is one that can accommodate your needs in a friendly and timely fashion. After all, you are not asking for their first born's head on a platter - merely that the sauce be left off your stir fry! The simple test I use is to order something with ingredients all mixed together, such as a stir fry and ask that the, mushrooms be left out. If they say no, then I know everything has been prepackaged and is not fresh. I pick out the mushrooms, as best I can, and don't go back.

Sometimes I get a little crazy and make a huge pot of vegetable soup, mixing rotation days together. It is glorious. I have broken the rules, not with a slab of chocolate layer cake, but with a thing as simple as soup. We all need to go a little crazy and break the rules - who said it has to hurt?

Everywhere you turn these days, experts are talking about phytochemicals as a way to beat health concerns ranging from cancer to the common cold. Research is showing that total wellness can be as simple as eating your fruits and vegetables, not as a side dish, but as the main course. How can we be so advanced and yet so backwards? People eat meat and cheese not because they should but because they can. The only link preventing certain diseases is the amount of fresh vegetables eaten - not race, nationality, gender or color. . . vegetables. So make meat and fish something you eat in moderation two or three times a week instead of two or three times a day and choose vegetables three times a day instead. A star is born - the organic veggie!

Creamy Watercress Soup

Don't let any one tell you, you can't enjoy delicious and satisfying creamed soups without dairy. This soup is wonderful, and you won't believe how easy it is to make. Not to mention the fat and calorie reduction from the original method. Watercress is such a delightful addition to a sandwich or salad. Please take a look at the variations. Also, the following cream soup variations will give you ideas for all four days of the rotation diet.

20 MINUTES TO PREPARE

2 SAUCE PANS, BLENDER OR FOOD PROCESSOR

CUTTING BOARD, KNIFE

STOVETOP ONLY

2 LARGE SERVINGS OR 4 SMALL

VARIATIONS

- If Watercress is out of season, use radish sprouts or parsley, kale, onion, garlic, horseradish or leeks. Artichoke hearts are also excellent.

- Other veggies that make a wonderful creamed soup are: parsnips, carrots, sweet potato, pumpkin, squash, split pea, great northern beans and avocado.

- Fresh herbs may also be used.

- Any chopped veggies may be used for the "chunky" portion of soup.

- Mashed cauliflower makes a wonderful mashed potato substitute.

Ingredients

- 1 small or 1/2 large Cauliflower (cut into pieces)
- 2 cups pure Water

- 2 cups chopped fresh Watercress
- 2 tablespoons extra virgin Olive oil
- 1 tablespoon Spike or another nutritional seasoning
- Sea Salt
- Fresh ground Pepper to taste
- 2 cups cubed Zucchini or Broccoli or Asparagus (or all three)

- reserved Watercress for garnish (optional)

PREPARATION

Place cauliflower and water in a 2 quart saucepan and cook for 10 minutes or until tender but do not over cook.

Once cauliflower is soft, reserve the water and gently mash cauliflower into a blender. Add enough of the water to process, once smooth continue to add the water until you reach the desired consistency of a creamed soup. Add remainder of ingredients and blend to chop vegetables into desired size. Taste and adjust seasoning at this time.

Pour soup into bowls, garnish with watercress. Serve at once.

SERVING SUGGESTIONS

This is best fresh since it does not freeze well, it is a good idea to only make what you can eat in a meal. Please adjust quantities accordingly. Very good with homemade crackers, see pages 66 - 67, 68 - 69 or Chapati 70-75 and a salad.

Spring Hash

I love all food. That is except Brussels sprout. I always thought they were interesting, looking like little cabbages, but I could never get past the way they tasted. My oldest son gave me this recipe and insisted I try it. Wow, he was right! The sweetness of the carrots and onions combine with the bite and texture of the sprouts to make this a delightful sensory experience. I find the early spring harvest of Brussels sprout to be the best tasting and most tender. Later in the season the vegetable tends to become a little tough and more bitter.

10 MINUTES TO PREPARE

10 MINUTES TO SAUTE

CUTTING BOARD, SHARP KNIFE

HEAVY SKILLET

SERVES TWO OR FOUR AS SIDE DISH

VARIATIONS

- Use broccoli or cabbage in place of the Brussels sprouts.
- For a tart bite add a squeeze of fresh lemon juice.
-
-
-
-

Ingredients

- 4 cups Brussels Sprout
- 4 large Carrots
- 1 bunch Green Onions
- 2 expeller pressed Coconut Oil
- Sea Salt to taste

PREPARATION

Wash and clean the vegetables. Cut the ends off of the Brussels sprouts and quarter them length wise. Set aside. Chop carrots into small pieces. I like to roll the carrot on the cutting board back and forth chopping at an angle as I roll. Chop green onions into half inch pieces 3 inches into the green.

Pour the coconut oil into a heavy skillet. Place all of the vegetables into the skillet and saute on high until just soft and brightly colored, about ten minutes. Salt to taste and serve at once.

SERVING SUGGESTIONS

Spring Hash can be the main course for breakfast, lunch or a side dish for dinner. This is so sweet and tasty. I love the texture.

Note: If you have tested positively for tree mix, avoiding raw carrots in the early spring and late fall is something to think about. Both raw carrots and celery cross react with tree pollen as do tree nuts.

Stuffed Artichokes

One of nature's most wonderful finger foods. I am always surprised when someone tells me they have never experienced eating a whole artichoke, (artichoke hearts don't count). This is a very relaxing sensual food, to be eaten slowly and savored. When choosing an artichoke look for large compact heads, if it feels light it will not be as flavorful as a heavier vegetable. Excellent as an elegant appetizer for a dinner party of close friends or just plain fun for the kids. . . any time you want to have a little sophisticated fun.

PREPARATION 5 MINUTES PER ARTICHOKE

30 - 45 MINUTES TO BOIL

SHARP KNIFE, CUTTING BOARD

GLASS OR STAINLESS STEEL STOVE TOP PAN OR GLASS BAKING DISH WITH A LID

1 ARTICHOKE PER PERSON

VARIATIONS

- Use this stuffing with cabbage leaves. Separate and wash cabbage leaves. Spread a thin layer of stuffing onto leaf (finely minced onion, garlic, celery, parsley, etc. may be added to stuffing). Roll jelly roll style and bake in a covered dish with a little water or No Tomato Marinara pages 122-123, till tender. Crumbs are also very good sprinkled over a spinach salad.
- Use a different grain for crumbs and/or oil.
- _____
- _____
- _____

Ingredients

- one Artichoke
- enough pure Water to cover 1/3 of vegetable
- pinch Sea Salt
- 1/2 cup Quinoa Cracker Crumbs, pages 66-67
- 1 tablespoon Olive oil

pages 66-67

DIPPING SAUCE: (OPTIONAL)

- 1/2 Lemon - juiced
- 2 tablespoons ex. v. Olive oil
- 1/4 clove Garlic minced
- Sea Salt and Black Pepper to taste

PREPARATION

Cut off all of stem and 1 inch from top of artichoke. With kitchen scissors snip tops from outer leaves, discard scraps and wash artichoke. Crush cracker crumbs as finely as possible. A food processor or blender may be used. If using a blender, grind 1/4 cup at a time. Using a dry, heavy skillet, toast crumbs until lightly browned and fragrant. Stir constantly, they will burn easily.

Fan leaves of artichoke as much as possible, evenly divide crumbs among leaves 'stuffing' each one. Drizzle top(s) with olive oil and place in a pan with a lid large enough to accommodate the number being cooked. Add a pinch of salt to enough water to cover 1/3 third of artichoke bottoms (be careful not to get any water on top of crumbs). Cover and boil 30 - 45 minutes or until an outer leaf pulls out easily; or may be baked in a 350° oven. Cooking time will depend on size of artichoke. Be sure to cover tightly.

Serve warm with dipping sauce, if you like, but it is not necessary.

DIPPING SAUCE: Using a jar with a lid combine lemon juice, olive oil, garlic, salt and pepper to taste. Shake well and serve with artichoke.

To eat, pull one leaf at a time out of heart, dip in sauce and scrape off meat and stuffing with your teeth, discard leaf. Continue until you come to the 'choke'. Scrape out the thorns and fuzz with a spoon and discard, dip and eat the heart. A warm wet towel should also be served. This is a personal favorite.

Broccoli Slaw

Broccoli is a member of the Cruciferous Family. Named by the early Spanish explorers, the delicate white flowers reminded them of a Crucifix. All members of this family are rich in anti-cancer compounds called indoles which may reduce colon cancer by as much as 70%. Some researchers feel this family of vegetables accelerates the metabolism of hormones speeding them out of the body, theoretically, reducing the possibility of hormone linked cancers.

30 MINUTES TO PREPARE

BLENDER

FOOD PROCESSOR (OPTIONAL)

KNIFE AND CUTTING BOARD

SERVES 2 TO 4

VARIATIONS

- All fruits and vegetables get "cooked" by the human digestive process. Raw is the best way to eat fruits and vegetables.
- Use shredded green and red cabbage in place of the broccoli.
- Add green onions or fresh chopped apple to the slaw and garlic to the dressing. Be creative.

- _____

- _____

- _____

Ingredients

SLAW
- 3 - 6 inch long thick stems of organic broccoli, pealed
- 3 large organic carrots
- 1/2 cup dried Goji berries (optional)

DRESSING
- 2 inch piece of fresh ginger peeled and sliced thin across the grain
- 2 tablespoons of raw organic almond butter (optional if allergic to tree nuts)
- 2 tablespoons of Udo's Choice Oil or XV Olive Oil
- Juice of one lemon (or for more bioflavanoids, use a peeled whole lemon)
- 8 drops liquid stevia or to taste
- 1 teaspoon sea salt
- 1/2 teaspoon toasted sesame oil
- 1 cup organic coconut milk

PREPARATION

Place all dressing ingredients in a blender and blend until smooth and creamy. Taste and adjust flavors. For thinner dressing add more coconut milk. Set aside.

Sometimes the grocer will have organic broccoli slaw premade, if so feel free to use that to save time and trouble. If not, shred or thinly slice broccoli stems and carrots, I use a food processor. In a large bowl mix with goji berries or any of the variations you wish. Add dressing and stir until well incorporated.

SERVING SUGGESTIONS

This is a wonderful use of the "once thrown away" sweet broccoli stems. An extremely alkalizing and tasty dish. Slaw will keep for 24 hours, but best if enjoyed right away.

Arame, Onions & Carrots

As a rule I do not recommend any thing but steam or a light saute for cooking vegetables. However, I make an exception for root vegetables - hearty, flavorful, and satisfying. These veggies may be roasted in the oven or sauteed on the stovetop, either way the result is wonderful. Caramelizing brings out all the sweetness in a vegetable. I have satisfied a sugar craving by simply over-cooking some carrots or beets.

15 Minutes to Prepare

30 Minutes on Stovetop

Cutting Board, Knife

Heavy Skillet with Lid

Serves Four

VARIATIONS

- Bake garlic in a small covered container for 45 minutes at 400° or until fragrant and brown. When done, it should spread like butter, use as you would butter.
- Stuff a large red onion with chopped veggies and 'bread' crumbs, bake until tender pages 106 - 107.
- Mix caramelized veggies with steamed veggies or raw veggies for an unusual and tasty stir fry.
- Peel and julienne beets and carrots, caramelize in olive oil and serve over rice noodles or mash and use as pate' with raw vegetables.
- Bake whole unpeeled beets in a close fitting covered baking dish for 2 - 2 $\frac{1}{2}$ hours at 400°. Remove from oven and when cool enough to handle, peel and slice thin. Serve drizzled with olive oil, salt, pepper and chopped mint or parsley.

Ingredients

- 2 Carrots cut into slices on a diagonal
- 2 Onions sliced thin
- 1 tablespoon Sesame oil
- 1 teaspoon toasted Sesame oil

- 2 cups Arrame (Sea Vegetable)
- 4 cups Water from a pure source

- 2 teaspoons fresh Lemon juice
- Sesame salt to taste.

PREPARATION

Soak Arame in water for 15 minutes, drain and rinse well. While soaking Arame prepare carrots and onion, saute vegetables in hot oil in a heavy skillet until tender, about 15 minutes. Place prepared Arame on top and continue to cook on low another 15 minutes. Do not stir, allow carrots and onions to caramelize on bottom and Arame to steam on top.

When done invert into a large bowl add lemon juice and sesame salt, gently toss.

Serve at once.

SERVING SUGGESTIONS

Arame is one of my favorite sea vegetables and is great hot or cold.

Fixed this way, it makes a very unusual and satisfying dish - warming on a cool day, energizing on a warm. This may also be served without the Arame. Excellent when combined with fresh raw vegetables.

Dressings

Flavor is a hard thing to give up - so why do it! In a world of gourmet vinegar you can feel like an outcast eliminating it from your diet. Vinegar is such a highly acid-forming food I do not recommend consuming it. The pH of vinegar is around 2.8. It takes a lot of your body's buffers to balance just a little vinegar. However, a little vinegar in warm water is great for cleaning floors and windows.

PREPARATION TIME A FEW MINUTES

BLENDER – MAY NEED STRAINER
OR SCRAPER

FRESH ORGANIC FRUITS & VEGETABLES

EACH RECIPE MAKES FOUR SERVINGS

THICKENERS

- If soy (some brands of tofu contain corn – call the manufacturer to be sure) is an option for you, Japanese style is an excellent choice for a creamy texture and mimics dairy quite well. Be sure to blend it into a creamy state before adding any other ingredients. Tofu may be substituted for any thickener. Tofu, lemon and horseradish make a great condiment. Try tofu, umeboshi plum paste and olive oil as a mayo substitute.

- Ground flax seeds also make a good thickener for sauces of all types.

- _____

- _____

Note: Preparation for all dressings on page 101.

Ingredients

BERRY DRESSING

- 1 cup fresh or frozen organic Raspberries or Strawberries
- 1/2 cup pure Water
- 1/2 cup Sunflower oil
- 1/2 teaspoon Sea Salt (optional)
- 1 teaspoon fresh grated Ginger

Excellent on a tossed green salad. Serve with fresh Spinach and whole Strawberries or over chilled cooked and cubed Beets.

HONEY MUSTARD

- 1 tablespoon Raw Honey or Agave Nectar
- Stevia to taste
- 1 yellow Summer Squash steamed till tender
- 1/2 teaspoon dry Mustard
- 1 tablespoon Coconut oil

Good served as a dip with veggies.

CREAMY LEMON

- Juice from 2 Lemons - seeded
- 1/4 cup extra virgin Olive oil
- 1 cup cooked Cauliflower - reserve water if needed to thin
- 1 teaspoon Bee Pollen
- 1 tablespoon Tarragon (if possible) snipped fresh
- Sea Salt and fresh ground Pepper to taste

Slice and saute Cauliflower in Canola oil until brown and tender, serve in a pool of dressing.

Ingredients

FRUIT TOPPER

- 1 tablespoon Flax seeds soaked for 15 minutes in 1-1/2 cups Apple, Pineapple, Grape or Orange juice. Mix thickened juice with...
- 1 tablespoon Lemon juice
- 1 tablespoon Poppy seeds (added after blended)

Chill and serve over fresh fruit salad for breakfast.

AVOCADO DRESSING

- 1 ripe Avocado
- Juice from 1 Lemon
- 1/2 cup Water from a pure source (more or less to adjust thickness)
- 3 drops liquid Stevia
- 2 Green Onions minced (added after blended)
- 1 tablespoon fresh minced Basil or Tarragon (added after blended)

Very good tossed with fresh bean sprouts

OIL & CITRUS

- Juice from one Lemon or Lime or 2 tablespoons Grapefruit juice
- 1/2 cup extra virgin Olive oil
- Sea Salt and fresh ground Black Pepper to taste

This topper works for almost anything and is perfect when eating out, every restaurant has oil and lemon.

ORANGE & SESAME SEED

- 1 cup fresh squeezed Orange juice
- 2 tablespoons raw hulled Sesame seeds

My favorite way to serve this is over shredded Carrots.

Breakfast

Pages 32-35 Pancakes & Waffles

Pages 48-49 Breakfast Salad

Pages 40-41 Blueberry Muffins

Pages 46-47
Green Smoothie

Pages 36-37
Sweet Breakfast
Smoothies

Pages 44-45 Very Berry Coffee Cake

Pages 42-43
Orange Muffins

Pages 38-39
Carob Breakfast Pudding

A

Yeast Free & Alternative

Pages 60-61
Savory Teff Cakes

Pages 40-43 & 152-155
Variety Muffin Basket

Page 56
Biscuits —
Buns —
Dumplings
Spelt Variation

Pages 78-79 Kamut Pumpkin Bread

Pages 68-69 Toasted Amaranth Rounds

Pages 70-75 Chapati

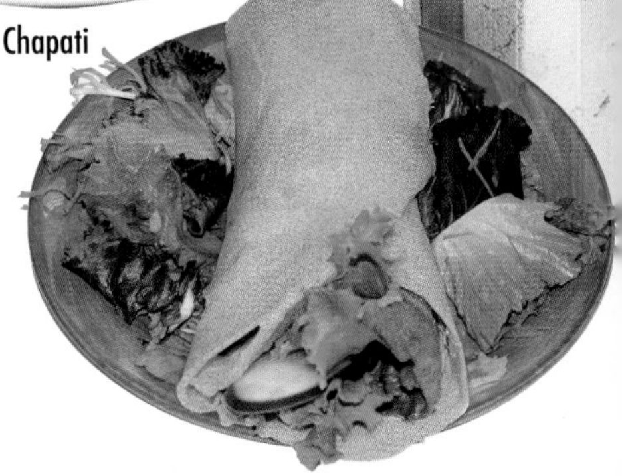

Grain Breads

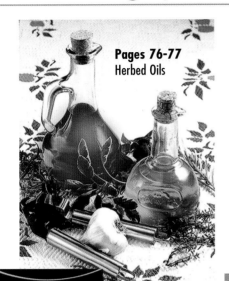

Pages 76-77
Herbed Oils

Pages 64-65
Spinach Bake

Page 55
Biscuits —
Buns —
Dumplings
Barley Variation

Pages 62-63 Bread Spreads

Pages 80-81
Spelt Olive Bread

Page 56
Biscuits — Buns — Dumplings
Rice Variation

Pages 66-67 Quinoa Crackers

Soups & Veggies

Pages 86-87
Creamy Watercress Soup

Pages 102-103
Creamy
Lemon Soup

Pages 108-109
Cream of No
Tomato Soup

Pages 88-89
Spring Hash

Pages 90-91
Stuffed Artichokes

Pages 94-95
Arame, Onions & Carrots

Pages 104-105
Three Bean
Salad

Pages 106-107
Stuffed Onion Bake

Pages 92-93
Broccoli Slaw

**Pages
96-101**
Dressings

D

Main Course Meals

Sweet Treats

Pages 142-143
Tapioca Pudding

Pages 156-157
Carob Cake

Pages 144-145
Almond Biscotti

Pages 164-167
Cake Toppers

Pages 148-149
Pear Tart

Pages 150-151
Plum Upside
Down Cake

Pages 162-163
Sorbet

Pages 168-173
Pie Crust

Sweet Treats

Pages 146-147
Pineapple Lemon Pie

Pages 158-159
Poached Pears

Pages 154-155
Basic Carob Brownies

**Pages
168-173**
Pie Crusts

Page 141
Easy Treats

Pages 152-153
Carrot Muffins
or Cakes

Pages 174-175
Sesame Candy

**Pages
160-161**
Sweet Oat Sauce

G

Eat Healthy!

As long as you
are alive it is
never too late
to feel healthy.

"Let your food
be your medicine and
let your medicine be
your food."
Hippocrates

Ingredients

HONEY GINGER

- 1 tablespoon Honey or Agave Nectar
- Few drops Stevia to taste
- Juice from 2 Lemons
- 1 tablespoon fresh ground Ginger
- 1/3 cup Sunflower oil
- 1/3 cup pure Water
- Sea Salt to taste

Omit water and use as a baste for barbecue.

MUSTARD

- 1/4 cup Apple juice
- 1/4 cup Canola oil
- 1/2 teaspoon dry Mustard
- 1/2 cup peeled and cored chopped Apple
- Sea Salt and fresh ground Black Pepper to taste

Good as a dipping sauce for steamed veggies.

CILANTRO & LIME

- 1/2 cup fresh Lime juice
- 1/2 cup Sesame oil
- 1/2 cup chopped Cilantro
- 1 tablespoon chopped Green Onion
- 1 teaspoon Sea Salt or Sesame Salt
- 6 drops liquid Stevia
- Pepper to taste (optional)
- For creamy dressing replace 1/4 cup Sesame oil for 1/4 cup Sesame Tahini

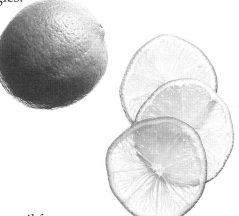

Wonderful over Zucchini Strips or as a marinade for chopped Celery and Carrots or a Sprouted Bean Salad.

Ingredients

TAHINI SAUCE

- 1/2 cup Sesame Tahini
- 1/2 cup pure Water
- 1/4 cup fresh Lemon juice
- 2 cloves Garlic minced
- 1/2 teaspoon Umeboshi Plum Paste

Excellent with Falafel page 124-125.

MANGO DRESSING

- 1 ripe Mango peeled and cubed
- 1/2 teaspoon fresh grated Ginger
- 1/2 teaspoon Cardamom
- 1/2 cup Sunflower oil
- 1 tablespoon minced Cilantro and/or Celery added after blended

Very good over a fruit or lettuce salad.

UME PLUM DRESSING

- 1 teaspoon Ume Plum Paste
- 1/2 cup Sesame oil or Olive oil
- 1/2 cup pure Water
- 1/2 cup chopped Parsley

Similar to a Vinaigrette dressing. Yummy over a Spinach or Avocado and Sunflower seed salad.

Ingredients

ORANGE POPPY SEED

- 1-1/2 cups fresh squeezed Orange juice
- 1 teaspoon finely shredded organic Orange peel
- 2 tablespoons fresh squeezed Lemon juice
- 1/3 cup Olive oil
- 1 teaspoon Poppy seed added after blended
- 1 tablespoon finely chopped green Onion (optional)

   Very good tossed with cooked cubed Sweet Potato.

PREPARATION

Choose set of ingredients and place in a blender. Process until mixed and refrigerate a couple of hours to combine flavors.

SERVING SUGGESTIONS

Experiment, these may also be used as a marinade for vegetables. Spice up rice, quinoa or pasta with one of these dressings or brush on biscuits or chapati.

Try this; Cook together 1/2 cup White Basmati Rice - 3/4 cup Brown Rice - 1/4 cup Long Grain Wild Rice with 3 cups pure Water, 2 Bay Leaves, 1 tablespoon Sesame oil and 1 teaspoon Sea Salt. Once cooked, add 1/2 cup chopped Green Onions, 1/2 cup frozen Peas, 1/2 cup chopped Parsley, 1 tablespoon minced Mint, 1/2 cup minced Celery, 1/2 cup dried Cranberries, 1/2 cup chopped Pecans. Combine all with Honey Ginger dressing and refrigerate to combine flavors at least 3 hours.

Make any substitutions or additions that suit your taste. I especially like Nigella seeds for both health and good taste. These little black seeds enhance most of the above dressings.

Note: Only use Stevia as a sweetener if on a Candida diet

Creamy Lemon Soup

Soup is so versatile, hot or cold, as a start to a meal or as the meal itself. Just about any old thing can be thrown into the pot and come out heavenly. When ever I cook or steam a vegetable I reserve the broth and freeze it, by the end of the week I have enough stock for a great bowl of soup. A couple of onions, a few herbs, throw in a few fresh veggies and wow! At the very least the broth can be used instead of plain water for cooking rice or quinoa.

30 MINUTES TO PREPARE
ALLOW UP TO 3 HOURS IF COOKING BEANS
CUTTING BOARD, KNIFE
SKILLET, LARGE SAUCE PAN, BLENDER
SERVES 4 - 6

VARIATIONS

- Use a different bean, navy, pinto, etc.
- Replace peppermint with a different herb, bay leaf is nice.
- Add a cup of frozen peas or another fresh vegetable to finished soup.
- Omit peppermint and replace olive oil with 2 tablespoons of sesame tahini and serve with toasted chapati rectangles page 62.

- _____
- _____
- _____

Ingredients

- 2 - 16 oz cans organic cooked Garbanzo beans, drained
- Juice from 1 large Lemon
- Sea Salt to taste

- 2 cups pure Water or
  Vegetable Broth
- 1 Peppermint Tea Bag or
  2 tablespoons fresh Peppermint

- 2 tablespoons extra virgin Olive oil
- 1 medium Yellow Onion diced
- 1-2 cloves Garlic minced

PREPARATION

Open, drain and rinse Garbanzo Beans. If cooking Garbanzo Beans from scratch, follow package directions and drain, reserving 4 cups beans. Bring water to a boil remove from heat and add peppermint or tea bag, while steeping, saute onion and garlic in olive oil till onion is translucent, remove tea bag.

Place 1 cup beans and 1/2 cup peppermint tea in blender and process till smooth, repeat 3 more times until all beans and tea have been used. Process onion, garlic and olive oil in last batch. If you have a VitaMix this may be done in one batch.

NOTE: Leave blender lid slightly ajar to allow steam to escape while processing any hot food. Steam builds rapidly and can explode out of the top causing a great mess and possible burns to anyone standing near.

Place all ingredients including lemon and sea salt in a sauce pan and heat through. Garnish with a lemon slice and sprig of mint.

SERVING SUGGESTIONS

You guessed it, this is great with a big salad!

Three Bean Salad

As a side dish or a main course, hot or cold. At home or as a dish to pass at a pot luck dinner. I love beans and this is a great way to enjoy them. If you have the time, soak and cook the beans yourself or if time is short, use canned. Remember my recipes are basic; look to the suggested variations for other additions that may agree with you. Please allow the extra day for soaking the beans, if cooking from scratch.

OVER NIGHT TO SOAK DRIED BEANS
SEVERAL HOURS TO COOK
10 MINUTES TO PUT TOGETHER
3 HOURS TO MARINATE OR STAND OVER NIGHT
SERVES 6

VARIATIONS

- Add chopped cucumbers, broccoli, peas, garlic, asparagus, etc.
- Use a different variety of beans. . . make a five bean salad. . . use sprouted beans in place of cooked – see page 82.
- Use herb other than mint. Tarragon is a good choice if avoiding the mint family or parsley or dill.
- Use lemon, lime, orange or pineapple juice in place of grapefruit.
- Throw in 2 cups cooked rice or spelt rotini pasta.

NOTE

If you have been avoiding beans because of "gas", no need. Most of the enzymes that cause this problem are in the soaking and cooking water. Be sure to discard all water after these two steps and beans will become your friend! Add drained, cooked beans to vegetable broth if making soup.

Ingredients

- 2 cups cooked Aduke Beans
- 2 cups cooked Black-eyed Peas
- One piece Kombu (optional)

- 2 cups frozen Green Beans cut into 1-$\frac{1}{2}$" pieces
- 1/2 cup chopped Red Onion
- 1/2 cup chopped Green Onion with tops
- 1/2 cup chopped Celery
- 1/2 cup chopped Parsley

MARINADE

- 1/2 cup chopped fresh Mint or 1/4 cup dried Mint
- 1 cup Grapefruit juice
- 1/2 cup Olive Oil
- 1 teaspoon Sea Salt adjust according to taste
- 6 drops liquid Stevia or to taste or 2 tablespoons of Agave Nectar

PREPARATION

If you do not have the time to cook your own beans use canned. If you do cook your own follow package directions and be sure to discard soaking and cooking water. A piece of kombu added at the start of cooking will tenderize the beans.

Drain cooked beans and mix with green beans, onions, celery and parsley. Make veggie variation choices, if any and add at this time. Mix together marinade ingredients and add to bean mixture, toss, cover and refrigerate over night or at the least 3 hours.

SERVING SUGGESTIONS

Serve warm with pine nuts and pasta. Throw in a food processor and serve as a dip for toasted Chapati wedges page 71.

Stuffed Onion Bake

One of my favorite truisims is by poet/author Carl Sandburg. To him, life is like an onion: "layer after perplexing layer that sometimes can make you cry." However, if you don't want to cry while slicing an onion, be sure to leave the root end intact, and never cut directly into it. Most of the onion vapor which reacts with tears and forms sulfuric acid is concentrated in the root portion. As far as life. . . you're on your own. If you figure it out please give me a call!

15 MINUTES EACH TO PREPARE

45 MINUTES TO BAKE

MELON BALLER, KNIFE, CUTTING BOARD

COVERED BAKING DISH & HEAVY SKILLET

OVEN TEMPERATURE 350°

ONE RECIPE PER PERSON

VARIATIONS

- Make an onion casserole, prepare extra stuffing and slice onion, alternate layers of stuffing and onion in a baking dish starting with onion and ending with stuffing. If you want something a little more hearty add layers of spinach or broccoli. Bake 350° for one hour.
- Stuff pearl onions and serve as an hors d'oeuvre or as a garnish, for color use red Italian onions.
- Chop onion and mix with stuffing and use to stuff a squash.
- _____
- _____

Ingredients

- One medium sized Yellow Onion peeled per person
- 1 Tablespoon Walnut or Olive oil
- 1/4 cup finely crumbled Yeast Free Spelt or Rice Bread
- 1/4 teaspoon each, Sage, Thyme, Rosemary and Basil
  (if possible use fresh or 1 tablespoon Poultry Seasoning mix)
- 2 tablespoons Water or Vegetable Broth
  (8 tablespoons equals 1/2 cup liquid)
- 1/4 cup chopped Walnuts or Sunflower seeds
- Chopped Chive as garnish (optional)

PREPARATION

Pre heat oven at 350°. Slice 1/2 inch off top of onion(s). Scoop out enough of the center layers to hold 3/4 cup stuffing, a melon baller works well. Slice enough off bottom of onion to sit upright, it should look like a bowl. Using a heavy skillet, saute onion 'bowl' in oil until slightly brown and translucent. Place in baking dish, add 1/4 cup water or vegetable broth per onion to bottom of dish, place in oven, cover and bake 15 minutes.

Using same skillet, saute chopped centers from onion and toast walnuts in oil, turn off heat. Add bread crumbs, add herbs and mix well. Moisten with water or broth and mix again.

Remove onion(s) from oven. Fill cavity of onion with prepared stuffing covering entire onion like a cap. Return to 350° oven uncovered for another 30 minutes. Done when onion is soft and tops are brown. If you wish, garnish with chives or a sprig of fresh basil. Serve warm.

SERVING SUGGESTIONS

Onions are so very good for you for so many reasons. Eat them often. Prepared this way, a plain meal will seem elegant. Serve them whole or quartered and fanned out on a plate, as an appetizer or side dish. Fill a large casserole with them and bring as a dish to pass. A lovely garnish.

Cream of No Tomato Soup

Thoughts of a hot, steaming bowl of cream of tomato soup with some fresh white bread and butter on the side brings back warm childhood memories. With this heartwarming variation I don't feel deprived and, even better, I don't feel sick for the next three days! For my white bread, I substitute Brown Rice bread and herbal oil in place of butter.

People have asked me many times if I'm sure there is no milk in this soup, I guarantee . . not if I've made it!

20 MINUTES TO PREPARE
CUTTING BOARD, KNIFE
4 GENEROUS BOWLS
BLENDER, SAUCE PAN

VARIATIONS

- Add a cup of cooked rice or rice pasta.
- Add chopped cooked veggies such as squash, broccoli, beans, okra, etc.
- Add chopped spinach for No Tomato Florentine.
- Serve chilled.
- Add fresh herbs.

Ingredients

- 1 large or 2 small raw Beets peeled and sliced
- 1 large Carrot sliced
- 1 small or 1/2 large head Cauliflower chopped
- 2 Bay Leaves broken
- 1/2 teaspoon Sea Salt
- 2 cups pure Water

- 2-3 stalks Celery diced

- 1 tablespoon Brown Rice Miso
  (made from soy optional) or
  Sea Salt to taste

PREPARATION

Place first six ingredients in sauce pan and cook until tender. Remove bay leaf pieces and add diced celery and cook additional two minutes. With a slotted spoon place beets, cauliflower and celery in a blender. Add enough of the remaining broth to blend until smooth. Continue to add broth until desired consistency is reached; if necessary, add more water. The miso does contain fermented soy and if you are sensitive to soy or have a raging candida overgrowth, use the sea salt to taste. Now is also a good time to add any fresh herbs you might wish to add. Blend one more time and serve.

SERVING SUGGESTIONS

Why not start off your day with a warming cup of this soup? Once you can break away from traditional menus your battle for better health is all but won. When we cook vegetables they become less alkaline. For balance be sure to include enough raw green foods in your day.

Why Green Is Good

Nothing corrects acid pH in the human body quite like green foods. I believe green foods were created for both our internal and external health and wellbeing. If you were to take a cell of chlorophyll and a cell of human blood and look at them under a microscope you would discover something very interesting. What you would see is that they are identical in their configuration. The only difference being the nucleus. The nucleus of the chlorophyll is magnesium making leaves green, while the nucleus of blood is iron making the blood red. Other than that they are the same. For me, that is a strong indication that the two are meant to be compatible with one another, the perfect complement. Leaves filter the air outside and green foods nourish and cleanse our internal environment as well.

When my boys were little, my favorite time of day was the reading of the bedtime story. We would finish every day with a recap of the day and a book. One of our favorite authors was Dr. Seuss. The book that sticks out in my mind was *Green Eggs and Ham*. In this book, Sam-I-Am mounts a determined campaign to convince another Seuss character to eat a plate of green eggs and ham. I have always identified with Sam-I-Am, in fact, it has become my life's work to convince people to eat green foods. "Would you like them here or there?" and quite often the reply I hear is, "I do not like them here or there! I would not like them anywhere! I do not like green eggs and ham! I do not like them, Deborah!"

It is then my job to gently help people understand that without green foods true wellness will continue to elude them. This is not a fad diet. I don't have a lot of initials attached to credentials after my name. I do not need a double blind study to know that when I eat a clean green alkalizing diet I feel good and when I eat processed acid-forming foods I feel crummy. This is basic mom common sense; breath clean air, drink pure water, eat organic green foods, and exercise to release toxins. Feed the cells of your body what they crave and they will do the work for you. No Ph. D., required. The End. Period. ∎

Main Course Meals

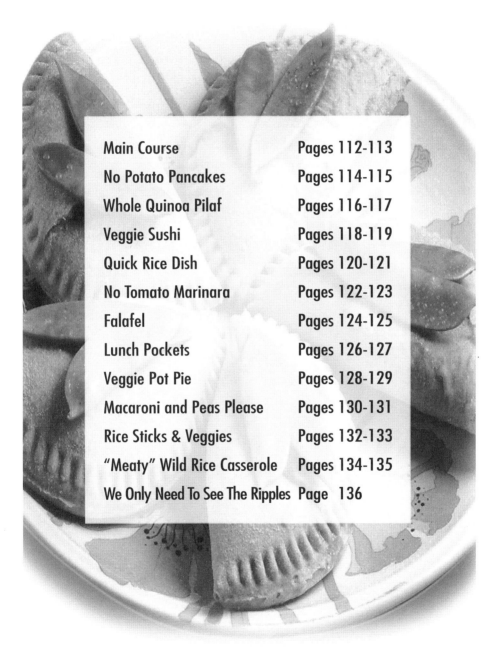

Main Course Meals

Make the companionship of friends and family the focus of a meal, not what's on the plate. I think the main reason I ate junk when at a party or restaurant was to be socially accepted by others. Instead of chips and dips, I look for the carrot sticks! If I know I am going someplace where my eating options are limited, I eat before I go. If I am not starving, I won't eat the wrong foods. There are three reasons we keep eating the same way: habit, to be socially accepted, and convenience. We think it's for the taste, but our taste buds have been so corrupted by sugar, dairy and MSG, we don't even know what real food should taste like.

Food should taste clean. In other words, when you put hollandaise sauce over asparagus, the vegetable is overpowered by the sauce. The delightful taste of crisp spring asparagus is lost. Your poor trusting taste buds shut down and before long you don't know what true food is.

Main Course Meals

When cooking dinner for people who choose not to follow your diet, a good strategy might be to fix your meal as a side dish. If you have been invited to someone else's home for dinner, offer to bring a  dish, and make sure it's something you can eat. Make something sensible but tasty and safe! Make the best choice you can in any given situation.

If you eat meat, choose natural meats or small cold water fish and keep the meal simple. Dinner may be the easiest meal of the day for you. If that's the case make it the start of your rotation day rather than breakfast. It doesn't matter where the 24 hours begins as long as you rotate and make an effort to eat as green as you can.

It is human nature to want everyone to be like you, to accept you and to be understanding. Unfortunately other people feel the same way, and since we are all different, the true meaning of life becomes clouded by ego and insecurity. The best advice I can give, is to stay true to yourself and the people you care about.

I hope you enjoy the following recipes as much as my friends and family do. Some will look familiar and some will be new. They are all 'clean'. Whole grains, beans and pasta are the perfect foil for fresh vegetables and a healthy lifestyle. Fresh air, simple exercise, good food and the companionship of friends and loved ones are the necessary ingredients for a long, healthy, happy life. After all, life is the main course, not the food.

No Potato Pancakes

One of the greatest shocks for me was the discovery that potatoes and tomatoes were closely related and that I was grossly allergic to the entire Nightshade Family. As you already know, potatoes are a staple in the standard American diet and difficult to cut out. My mother still says, "what could possibly be in a potato that would make anybody sick". I'm sure most of America's moms agree with mine. How could something they so lovingly prepared be making their family suffer? So when you crave potatoes, try this safe alternative!

30 Minutes to Prepare

15 Minutes to Bake at 400°

10 Minutes Per Batch to Crisp on Stove

Food Processor Recommended & Heavy Skillet

Serves 4

VARIATIONS

- The addition of chopped veggies make these great "burgers".
- Use different seeds and nuts.
- Add fresh tarragon or another fresh herb.
- Leftovers may be frozen and thawed in toaster.

- _____
- _____
- _____

Ingredients

- 1 cup whole organic Quinoa - washed and cooked in 1-3/4 cup pure Water
- 1/2 cup hulled ground Sunflower seeds
- 1/4 cup Tapioca flour
- 1/2 teaspoon Sea Salt
- 3 tablespoons whole Flax seeds
- 2 tablespoons Sunflower or Coconut oil per batch

- Flour & Oil for cookie sheet

PREPARATION

Cook quinoa according to package directions. Be sure to wash bitter outer coating off of the grain or it will taste bitter.

Place cooked quinoa and all other ingredients (except flour & oil for cookie sheet) into a food processor. Blend until a ball forms, you will need to stop and scrape sides once or twice. Lightly oil and flour cookie sheet. If you do not have a food processor, place all ingredients except whole quinoa in a blender and process. Mix with whole quinoa and mash the mixture with the bottom of a non-breakable cup in the bowl, as you would with a mortar and pestle. Using your hands (it will be very sticky) form into approximately 1/4 cup patties. Place on a prepared cookie sheet. Bake in a 400° preheated oven for 15 minutes, if you omit this step the cakes will soak up the oil like a sponge and be too oily.

Pour oil into heavy skillet or griddle. Fry cakes until golden on bottom, flip over and press flat with a spatula. Serve once both sides are golden.

SERVING SUGGESTIONS

Great with a salad pages 48-49 and Stuffed Artichoke, pages 90-91.

Whole Quinoa Pilaf

We have become accustomed to rice being the only grain used in a whole grain form. What a shame. All of the grains may be eaten and enjoyed whole. Quinoa is my personal favorite, for texture, taste and nutritional value, it is unsurpassed. Quinoa can easily stand in for rice or couscous, hot or cold. Whether it's a quick fix for a cool night main course, or as a tasty side dish, whole grain quinoa will become a family favorite.

10 MINUTES TO PREPARE

15 - 20 MINUTES TO COOK

CUTTING BOARD, KNIFE

1-1/2 QUART SAUCE PAN WITH LID

HEAVY SKILLET

SERVES 4 AS A SIDE DISH

VARIATIONS

- Add 1 cup sliced black olives
- Add 1/4 cup each, chopped green onions, mint, parsley and water chestnuts, toss with Cilantro & Lime Dressing page 99. Chill and serve.
- Combine ingredients from other days of the rotation, example brown rice or millet, slivered almonds, sesame seeds, parsley and dill with sesame oil – or toasted buckwheat groats, toasted pumpkin seeds and kale with canola oil – or kamut, walnuts, peas, onion, garlic and basil with olive oil, etc.

Ingredients

- 1 cup whole grain Quinoa uncooked
- 1-3/4 cups pure Water
- 1 tablespoon Sunflower oil
- 1/2 teaspoon Sea Salt

- 1/2 cup hulled Sunflower seeds
- 1 tablespoon Flax seeds
- 1 cup finely minced Spinach

PREPARATION

Wash quinoa in cool water to remove bitter outer coating (if you do not do this, it will be too bitter to eat) drain. Place in pot with water, oil and salt, bring to a boil, cover with lid and turn heat down to a simmer for 15 minutes or until all water is absorbed.

While quinoa is cooking, prepare other ingredients. In a dry heavy skillet toast sunflower seeds until golden. Mince fresh spinach.

Combine all ingredients, cover and allow to rest 10 minutes. Serve hot or chilled.

SERVING SUGGESTIONS

Serve in a bed of fresh spinach leaves with quartered artichoke hearts on the side, drizzle all with Herbed Sunflower Oil pages 76-77 and Tarragon.

Veggie Sushi

Believe it or not this is great for a bag lunch. If allowed to cool several hours, the colorful little rolls will transport well. If you have been avoiding wheat this can be a creative way to skirt the whole sandwich issue. I find bread to be more of a convenience/habit than anything. Using leftover rice from dinner, these are as easy to make as a sandwich. In fact many people following a rotation diet start their 24 hour period with dinner, so that the leftovers can become lunch or breakfast.

1 HOUR TO PREPARE

CUTTING BOARD, SHARP KNIFE

SAUCE PAN, STOVETOP

WAX PAPER

SERVES 2-4

VARIATIONS

- The grain needs to be sticky, therefore a sticky rice works best and most substitutions will crumble.
- Other veggies may be used, try to stick to colorful vegetables chopped to work in this format. Example; watercress, cucumber, beets or sprouts.
- Use another sauce from Dressings pages 96 through 101, or a preservative free bottled sauce or dressing or perhaps some ground ginger.
- Cook rice with a broken bay leaf (remove to serve) for added flavor, or add a tablespoon of fresh minced parsley to the cooked rice for color and flavor.

- Multiply recipe accordingly. A whole bag of nori is enough to feed a crowd.

-

Ingredients

- 2 sheets Nori (sea vegetable)
- 2 cups cooked Short Grain Brown Rice or Sushi Rice
- 1 teaspoon Umeboshi Plum Paste
- 1 large Carrot cut into matchsticks
- 1 Avocado cut into matchsticks
- 6 fresh Spinach leaves washed with stems removed
- 1/4 cup or Jicama cut into matchsticks

PREPARATION

Place each sheet of nori on a square of unbleached wax paper, or sushi mat. Divide warm rice between the two sheets of nori and evenly distribute over top of each sheet. Place three of the spinach leaves across the bottom of the short end of each nori and rice sheet, overlapping just to the edges. Divide the carrot matchsticks between the two sheets and place on top of the spinach. Do the same with the avocado, jicama sticks and plum paste. To easily spread plum paste, place in a plastic sandwich bag, cut a small hole in one corner of bag and squeeze onto spinach. If avoiding plastic you may use a cloth pastry bag.

Starting at the spinach and carrot end of the nori begin to roll all layers like a jelly-roll. Use the wax paper to help guide an even tight roll, be sure not to include the wax paper or mat in the roll. Store in wax paper until ready to cut. Discard paper before slicing.

Allow to cool seam side down. Once cool, using a sharp knife with a serrated edge, cut into 1" slices. Serve with Tahini Sauce, page 100 for dipping or 1/4 cup Bragg's™ (soy), 1/4 cup Orange juice, 1 teaspoon ground fresh Ginger & 1 tablespoon Honey or Agave nectar mixed together. These are beautiful.

SERVING SUGGESTIONS

This is a show stopper as a dish to pass at a party. Sushi also make a great hors d'oeuvre or appetizer. If you wish, poach a whole fish to serve to company, add these little rolls to make an elegant accompaniment.

Quick Rice Dish

This is the perfect name for the following recipe, because it is quick, it's made with rice and what a dish. Whether you need to bring a dish to pass or have had a long day and need to put dinner together fast, this works. Good hot or cold, as a side dish or main course, lunch or dinner (even breakfast). In the time it takes to boil the rice you will create a wonderful and hearty meal.

30 MINUTES TO PREPARE

STOVETOP, POT, BLENDER,

BOWL, CUTTING BOARD, KNIFE

SERVES 4

VARIATIONS

- Use chick peas, sprouted aduki beans or another type of bean.
- Chop other veggies into the mix, carrots, broccoli, water chestnuts, etc.
- Use fresh herbs that agree with you.
- Add chopped nori or another sea vegetable.
- Make for a crowd, easy to double or triple recipe.

- _____

- _____

- _____

Ingredients

- 1/2 cup each White Basmati Rice and Brown Rice
- 2 tablespoons Wild Rice
- 2-1/4 cup pure Water
- 1/4 teaspoon Sea Salt
- 1 tablespoon Sesame oil

- One - 16 oz. can organic Aduki, drained and rinsed
- 3 large stalks Celery, chopped
- One small red Onion, chopped
- 1/2 cup chopped fresh Parsley

- 1/2 cup Sesame Tahini
- 1/4 cup extra virgin Olive oil
- Juice from one Lemon
- 2 tablespoons fresh Tarragon (2 teaspoons dried)
- 1 cup pure Water
- 1/4 teaspoon Sea Salt or Umeboshi Plum Paste to taste

PREPARATION

Combine first five ingredients in a 2 qt. covered glass or non-reactive pot. Bring to a boil, then reduce heat and simmer for 30 minutes or until all water is gone. If you have the time, allow to rest for another 10 minutes with the lid on.

While rice is cooking prepare the next four ingredients and place in a serving bowl.

Combine next six ingredients in a blender and process until combined and creamy.

When rice is done add to beans, celery, onion and parsley in the serving bowl. Pour Tahini Sauce over top and combine well.

SERVING SUGGESTIONS

Serve in a lettuce boat. Good hot or cold. Healthy acid-forming balance with raw veggies.

No Tomato Marinara

What can I say - I'm an Italian allergic to tomatoes, cheese and wheat. This sauce over brown rice pasta satisfies my craving. It looks and tastes enough like the real thing to fool anyone.

With all the genetic altering being done to tomatoes this is probably a much safer alternative to the original sauce. . . . forgive me grandma!

30 MINUTES TO PREPARE

CUTTING BOARD, KNIFE, GARLIC PRESS

20 - 25 MINUTES TO COOK

LARGE PASTA POT, 4 QUART SAUCE PAN

SERVES 4 TO 6

VARIATIONS

- Add two cups rice beverage or unsweetened soy milk or any cream alternative and serve as a creamy soup. Example: Creamy Watercress Soup from pages 86 & 87.
- Serve over spaghetti squash, brown rice pasta, quinoa noodles, spelt or kamut pasta, whole brown rice or quinoa, etc.
- Use as a sauce for a pizza on top of a crust made from a Chapati recipe pages 70-75, add veggies and enjoy.

- _____
- _____
- _____

Ingredients

- 1 Butternut squash or other squash with orange flesh or 1 pound carrots.
- 1 Beet without greens
- 2 Bay Leaves, broken
- 1 qt. pure Water

- 1 - 2 cloves Garlic minced
- 1 medium yellow Onion minced
- 2 tablespoons extra virgin Olive oil
- Sea Salt and fresh ground Pepper to taste
- Juice from 1/2 Lemon

- 1/2 cup chopped fresh Basil or 2 tablespoons dried
- 2 tablespoons chopped fresh Oregano or 1 teaspoon dried
- 1/2 cup chopped fresh Parsley or 2 tablespoons dried

PREPARATION

Cut squash in half, place cut side down on a cookie sheet and bake 30 minutes in a 350° pre heated oven. Cool to handle, peel and cube, or peel and cube one pound carrots. Peel and cube beet. Place squash or carrots, beet and bay leaf in large pot with enough water to cover all pieces and cook till tender, about 20 minutes. While cooking, saute onion and garlic in olive oil till translucent. Remove bay leaf and place all ingredients, except lemon juice, in blender or food processor and process until well combined and desired texture is achieved. Return to pot and cook another 10 minutes to combine flavors. Add lemon juice to taste and serve.

SERVING SUGGESTIONS

Serve as you would a tomato marinara sauce over fresh spinach and minced raw garlic with olive oil.

Falafel

This recipe is so satisfying. One of my favorite ways to eat food is in the form of a sandwich. Falafel fits the bill with a Middle Eastern flair. I sometimes use *Rudi's Spelt Pita Bread*, (it contains yeast) instead of fresh Chapati, see pages 70-75.

However, these may be eaten as 'meat' balls, or as finger food dipped in Tahini Sauce, page 100.

20 MINUTES TO PREPARE

20 MINUTES TO BAKE PLUS 20 TO FRY

COOKIE SHEET & HEAVY SKILLET

OVEN TEMPERATURE 375°

16 SMALL PATTIES

VARIATIONS

- Substitute or remove any herb you can not tolerate.
- Do not flatten balls into patties. Instead, use as you would 'meatballs' in a favorite sauce or in No Tomato Marinara, pages 122-123.
- Serve as an hors 'd oeuvre with vegetables and Honey Ginger Dressing on page 99.
- Make patties larger and serve as you would a hamburger with all the trimmings on a non wheat bun.
- Instead of making the chickpeas from scratch, use garbanzo flour or organic canned chic peas.
-
-

Ingredients

- 3 cloves Garlic chopped
- 1/2 Onion chopped
- 1/2 cup minced fresh Parsley
- 1-1/2 cups cooked Chickpeas
- 1 tablespoon fresh Lemon juice
- 1 teaspoon ground Cumin
- 1/2 teaspoon Sea Salt
- 1/2 tsp. each Basil, Coriander and Thyme
- 1/2 teaspoon Hot Pepper Sauce (optional nightshade)
- Black pepper to taste
- 2 cups Yeast Free Rice Bread torn into large pieces and soaked in cold water. . . squeeze out all water before using.
- 1/2 cup Rice flour
- 1 tablespoon extra virgin Olive or Coconut oil - per batch

PREPARATION

Preheat oven to 375°. Mince first three ingredients in food processor. Add cooked chickpeas and process until pasty. Add next seven ingredients and continue to process, stopping as needed, to scrape the sides of the bowl until well mixed.

Divide mixture into 16 balls and flatten. Dip into rice flour and bake at 375° oven 10 minutes on each side.

Place half tablespoon oil in a heavy skillet and fry patties until golden. Flip and do the same on the other side. Continue until all are fried.

SERVING SUGGESTIONS

Serve in spelt pita pockets cut in half or fresh spelt or rice chapati folded in half. Garnish with Tahini Sauce, page 100, sprouts, avocado, chopped onion, lettuce and/or cucumber — you choose.

Note: I do not recommend omitting the baking step. Without baking, the falafel will soak up all of the oil.

Lunch Pockets

I won fourth place in a Vita Spelt, national recipe contest with a version of this recipe years ago. These are wonderful in a bag lunch, made in advance and frozen for a later use. They are the perfect 'fast food'. The variations are endless, I will give some suggestions, but I encourage you to experiment. When my son was little he loved lunch pockets.

30 Minutes to Prepare

20 Minutes to Bake

Soak Beans Overnight or Use Canned

Large Skillet & Cookie Sheet

Cutting Board, Knife

Oven Temperature 425°

12 Pockets

VARIATIONS

- Make crust using any of the Chapati recipes pages 70-75.

- Fill with cubed zucchini, onion and No Tomato Marinara pages 122-123. Perhaps diced carrots, celery, water chestnuts, parsley and dill tossed with Cilantro & Lime dressing page 99.

- Make dessert pockets and fill with fruit or chopped nuts and maple sugar. How about mango and fresh ginger tossed with lime juice and honey or agave nectar.

- _____

- _____

- _____

Ingredients

- One recipe Spelt (non hybrid wheat) or Rice Chapati pages 72-73.
- 2 cups mixed cooked Beans (Kidney, Navy, Black, Garbanzo, Lima or any single Bean or mix you prefer)
- 1 cup fresh or frozen Peas
- 1 tablespoon extra virgin Olive oil
- 2 cloves Garlic minced
- 1 Leek chopped (about 4" into the green)
- 1 small Onion chopped
- 1 tablespoon dried Basil or 3 sprigs fresh
- 1 teaspoon dried Thyme or 2 sprigs fresh
- 1/2 teaspoon dried Oregano or 1 sprig fresh
- 1 teaspoon Sea Salt
- Herbed Olive Oil pages 76-77 to brush on top (optional)

PREPARATION

Prepare beans according to package instructions, a pre-packaged soup mix works well (do not use the spice pack), or use canned. While beans are in their last hour of cooking prepare Chapati dough according to directions and divide into 12 equal balls and flatten. Place unbleached wax paper in between each round and invert bowl over top to keep moist. Saute garlic and leek in olive oil till translucent. When beans are ready, combine with peas, garlic and leek, and next five ingredients.

In centers of dough, place equal amounts (about 1/4 cup) of bean mixture. Fold dough over and seal by moistening half of the edge with water and crimping with the tines of a fork or with fingers. Make three small slits in top and place on cookie sheet. Bake in a preheated 425° oven for 20 minutes or until golden, brush tops with herbed oil. Serve hot or at room temperature.

Note: Most of the gas from beans is in the water. Always discard soaking and cooking water.

Veggie Pot Pie

Hot and hearty is a good description of a Pot Pie. This has always been my favorite way of dealing with left-overs. Make a sauce, slice, dice and throw it all into a pie crust! I think when my oldest son was little, he looked forward to Thanksgiving next day pot pie, more than the original feast. With this recipe the same holds true. It 's a great way of dealing with perishable odds and ends in the fridge. The best part is it can be frozen and served another day.

30 MINUTES TO PUT TOGETHER

60 MINUTES TO BAKE IN A 375° OVEN

2 QT. COVERED POT, WHISK

BAKING DISH, 8" PIE PLATE,
FOOD PROCESSOR/BLENDER

SERVES 4

VARIATIONS

- Saute onions, garlic, celery, parsley, etc. and add to filling mix.
- Combine ingredients from other days of your rotation and use a coordinating flour pie crust. See pages 168-173.
- Use left-overs or make individual pies.
- Cut zucchini in half scoop out centers, steam for 5 minutes, and fill 'boats' with veggie filling, top with creamed cauliflower and bake.
- _____
- _____
- _____

Ingredients

- 1/2 recipe batter, Toasted Amaranth Rounds, pages 68-69.
- 1 tablespoon Poppy seeds or Nigella seeds
- Canola oil for pan
- 1/2 large Cauliflower head cooked in 2 cups pure Water (reserve water)
- 1/4 cup + 2 tablespoons Arrowroot powder divided
- 1 cup each Broccoli, Zucchini and Acorn Squash
- 1 teaspoon dry Tarragon - or - 1 tablespoon fresh
- Sea Salt and fresh ground Black Pepper to taste (optional)

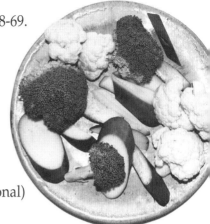

PREPARATION

Cut acorn squash in half, place face down on baking dish in 1/2" of water and place in 375°oven for 30 minutes. Hold squash until crust is ready — share oven time. Prepare amaranth dough according to directions. Oil bottom and inside edges of pie pan, sprinkle even layer of poppy or nigella seeds. Evenly spoon a layer of dough on bottom of pan. It will be sticky, moisten fingers with water and work dough up edges and smooth evenly on bottom. A second crust may be made at this time to freeze, or the second half of dough may be made into Toasted Amaranth Rounds. Share oven with squash. Bake together for 30 minutes. Remove squash and crust from oven.

While crust and squash are baking, prepare filling. In a covered pot, steam cauliflower in water till tender, about 10 minutes. Reserve water for sauce. Place cauliflower pieces in food processor with 1/4 cup arrowroot, add salt. Process until smooth and creamy. Cut broccoli and zucchini into 1/2 inch cubes, peal and cube cooked squash.

With a wire whisk blend 2 tablespoon arrowroot into cauliflower broth until there are no lumps. Return to heat and simmer, stirring constantly, until thick and smooth. Add tarragon, salt and pepper, simmer another minute. Adjust flavors to taste. Add broccoli, zucchini and squash to sauce combine well and pour into baked crust. Top with mashed cauliflower and return to 375° oven for another 30 minutes. Allow to rest for 30 minutes before serving.

Macaroni and Peas Please

Pasta is a perfect example of how limiting the Standard American Diet can be. The way I see it, before I discovered alternative grains, I only ate one kind of pasta — wheat. Now I eat a dozen truly different varieties, not just shapes. This recipe is good for family members who aren't quite ready to

go to all greens, but are willing to try something new, this is very kid friendly. The variations are endless. Once you start experimenting you will see what I mean.

20 Minutes to Prepare

Large Sauce Pan and Bowl

Serves 4

VARIATIONS

- Use a different shape or grain for pasta. Substitute with spaghetti squash or raw zucchini 'noodles'.
- Use a different oil, try a sesame and toasted sesame blend.
- Use a different veggie or assortment of vegetables. I like fresh organic sugar snap peas or add cooked beans, raw vegetables, onions raw or cooked in olive oil with a hint of garlic, olives, nuts, seeds, sauteed fresh kale or spinach. . . (see what I mean)
- Toss in a fresh herb, basil or tarragon or use an Herbed Oil pages 76-77.
- Toss in a dressing pages 96-101.
-

Ingredients

- 2 cups uncooked Macaroni or Shell
  or Rotini shaped Rice Pasta · GLUTEN-FREE

- 1 cup frozen Peas
- 1/2 cup minced Green Onions
- 1/2 cup minced Celery

- 1 teaspoon extra virgin Olive oil
- 6 sprigs fresh Parsley, any variety
- Vegi-Sal to taste or a suitable
  seasoning

PREPARATION

Cook pasta according to package
directions, drain. Combine with frozen
peas. Allow to rest one minute. Toss
with remaining ingredients. Adjust
flavors. May be served hot or chilled.

SERVING SUGGESTIONS

This has everything you need for a quick one
course meal. When served with spaghetti and still
warm from the garden tomatoes (nightshade) and
fresh basil, this is a to-die-for meal! Chilled primavera
isn't shabby either. What can I say - I'm Italian, and I
love pasta any way I can get it! Good dinner or lunch when
the cupboard is getting bare.

Rice Sticks & Veggies

I have found this to be one of the safest things to order in a Chinese restaurant. Because everything on the menu is a combination of the same ten ingredients or so, it is easy to custom order. Ask for rice sticks pasta and mixed vegetables, no mushrooms, soy sauce or MSG please. If there is a safe sauce on the menu have the kitchen use it or bring your own. The following is my at-home version. I absolutely love the texture of these chewy noodles.

20 MINUTES TO PREPARE

CUTTING BOARD, KNIFE

LARGE SAUCE PAN, KNIFE
SKILLET FOR STIR FRYING

SERVES 4

VARIATIONS

- Same variations as Macaroni & Peas Please page 130.
- I use Bragg™ Liquid Aminos (made from soy but not fermented) for this recipe. If you are unable to eat soy substitute sauteed onions with a hint of garlic and a 1/2 teaspoon of toasted sesame oil, the fresh ginger and stevia may then be added. Set this mix aside and follow rest of recipe directions.

- _____

- _____

- _____

Ingredients

- 1 package Rice Sticks cooked according to package directions - do not over cook

- 1/2 cup minced cilantro or parsley
- 6 Carrots
- 4 stalks Celery
- 3 green onions sliced thin

- 2 teaspoons fresh ground Ginger or to taste (I use a garlic press)
- 2 garlic cloves minced (I use a garlic press)
- 2 tablespoons Sesame oil
- 1/4 teaspoon toasted Sesame oil
- 1 teaspoon Bragg Liquid Aminos™ (soy) or use Sea Salt to taste.

PREPARATION

Clean carrots and slice on a diagonal while rolling carrot on cutting board. Clean celery and cut thin slices on a diagonal with stalk round side up. Small slivers of vegetables will work best with the fine texture of the noodles.

Mix together ginger, garlic and sesame oils. Saute until garlic is fragrant, about two minutes. Add carrots and celery and cook another couple of minutes.

In a large serving bowl toss cooked and drained rice sticks, all vegetables and sauce. Add Bragg's™ or sea salt, adjust flavors and serve at once.

SERVING SUGGESTIONS

Eat hot for dinner and eat cold leftovers for lunch the next day.

"Meaty" Wild Rice Casserole

I love wild rice. It has a nutty, meaty texture that is quite satisfying. I introduced this dish to my family around Halloween one year. I took a small organic pie pumpkin, scooped out the seeds and cut a jack-o-lantern face. Stuffed the pumpkin with the rice mixture and baked until the pumpkin was melt-in-your-mouth tender (about an hour and a half at 350°). The young and the young at heart will smile when this dish is the centerpiece to a candy-free Halloween feast. Be sure to toast the pumpkin seeds for snacking later on. This meal will be good twice, because no one will have a sugar hangover the next day.

NON-REACTIVE 3 QUART
SAUCE PAN WITH A LID

40 MINUTES TO PREPARE

40 MINUTES TO BAKE

CUTTING BOARD, KNIFE

9" x 13" GLASS BAKING DISH OR
CASSEROLE DISH

SERVES 4

VARIATIONS

- Acorn squash, pie pumpkin or omit the squash and use rice mix to make cabbage rolls.
- In place of dried cherries and almonds, use a chopped fresh apple with pecan pieces. If on a strict candida diet use no fruit.
- Substitute sliced water chestnuts if avoiding tree nuts. If soy is not a problem for you, Earth Balance™ non-hydrogenated spread in place of the oil for a more buttery taste.

Ingredients

- 1 cup Wild Rice
- 3 cups Water from a pure source
- 1/2 cup slivered raw Almonds
  (omit if sensitive to tree nuts)
- 1/2 cup sulfite and sugar-free dried
  tart Cherries
- 6 Green Onions chopped, greens included
- 1/2 cup minced fresh Parsley
- 1 medium Butternut Squash peeled, seeded
  and cut into 1" cubes
- 1 teaspoon non-irradiated ground Cinnamon
- 1/4 cup extra virgin Olive Oil
- 1 teaspoon Sea Salt or to taste

PREPARATION

Combine rice and water in a sauce pan with a lid. Bring to a boil, turn down heat and simmer for 40 minutes with lid on until rice is tender. While cooking rice, prepare all other ingredients and pre-heat oven at 375°. When rice is done combine all ingredients and place in baking dish cover with lid. If the casserole has no lid use a cookie sheet to cover. Bake for 40 minutes or until squash is tender. You may serve in a lettuce leaf for presentation.

SERVING SUGGESTIONS

Warming on a cold winter's night or great chilled for a 4th of July bar-b-que dish to pass.

Great served with a pomegranate and red leaf lettuce salad.

We Only Need to See the Ripples

To eat or what not to eat, that is the question. I think if there has been one reoccurring theme from our customers it has been; I am on the program, but my husband only wants meat and potatoes. All I can say is you are not alone. My own husband struggles with eating healthy. I don't have a reason, I just know it's a pattern. When we travel on an airplane we are told if there is a drop in cabin pressure, to place the air mask on ourselves first. We are of no use to anyone else if we ourselves are out of commission. We can't help our children, our aging parents, our friends and relatives... or our husbands if we are sick and tired.

Children of all ages learn by what they see. We can council, lecture, tell, inform or use any adjective we want, it is what people see and experience that makes the difference. Be the example. You set the bar for those you love. Trust me, when everyone sees your transformation, they will want whatever it is you have been doing. Children will eat whatever is in the refrigerator and pantry. Yes, I guarantee they will cheat when they are out of the home. That's alright. They will soon make the connection to how crummy they feel eating junk. Our children are wiser than we give them credit. My now adult oldest son taught me that children do listen and observe, they just don't want you to know. As an adult he now practices very high eating standards, but that was not always the case. Growing-up he caused me great anguish, it was his hobby.

Look to nature for all answers. Lessons for our inner world play out in nature. Even the hardest rock surrenders its sharp edges to the wind and the rain. It's your actions not your words that will move mountains. Subtle changes will start to make a difference. Serve a tasty vegetable dish with the meat and potatoes. When you make the morning coffee replace a fourth of the ground coffee with an alkaline natural coffee substitute such as Teeccino™. Put a tablespoon of dried wheat grass powder in the meat loaf and use rice bread crumbs. When you make dishes that call for milk use rice or fresh almond milk instead. Just the switch to organic will help. Use a laundry ball for both the washer and the dryer. Eliminate toxins in the home. No soda pop in the house. Quietly and purposefully make the little changes that will make a big difference. No one needs to know. One of my grandmother's favorite bits of advice was, "a man doesn't need to know everything". We don't need to see the drop of water hit the pond, we only need to see the ripples to know the drop exists. ∎

Sweets & Treats

Sweets & Treats

When my family first began eating this new way, the thing we craved most was (of course) goodies. In my naivete, I replaced cane sugar with gallons of maple syrup and honey. Concentrated fruit juice became my best friend. Raisins and dried fruit were tossed into everything. No wonder our conditions became worse. Until you have consulted a qualified health care professional or done a great deal of research, don't assume anything.

My mistake, made out of ignorance, was two fold. First we had replaced one allergen with others and secondly, we suffered from a Candida overgrowth which grew out of control quickly. Let me take a minute to discuss Candida.

Candida albicans is the biological name for a common yeast that is found in the mucous membrane of the gastrointestinal and genitourinary tract. The Candida organism normally lives in harmony with the human body. However, it is an opportunistic organism, which means that it will try to establish a greater territory by growing and expanding its presence in the tissues. Once overgrown, it can wreak havoc with all of our body functions. When the body's immune system is weakened Candida can invade the tissue, take over residence and colonize outside of the gastrointestinal tract. Causes of Candida or yeast overgrowth are varied. It can be passed at birth from an infected mother to her child, use of broad spectrum antibiotics, birth control pills, immunosuppressant drugs (Cortisone and Prednisone), or a sugary over-processed diet and stress are only some of the causes.

Once Candida takes hold it is difficult to get your body back into check, you may need the help of a qualified health care professional. Also, please take a look at the helpful books and products on my website www.feelgoodfood.com or call for a free catalog. Foods that aggravate the condition are ALL sweets, ALL yeasts, ALL ferments, ALL dairy and ALL molds.

A short list of foods containing these items are soy sauce, yeasted, breads, tempe, mushrooms, cheese, vinegar, fruit juice, dried fruit, sweets, and ALL foods containing

them, to name a few. Even chemicals used to bind fragrances to products and polyester can aggravate the condition.

Yes, I know that in some of the following recipes I use poor food combining and some call for cooked fruit. This next section is intended for occasional use and is transitional. All of the recipes are "better choices" not "perfect choices". Try to eat them alone or with a salad meal. Bring with to a party or serve at holiday gatherings or when the cravings are so bad it is the only thing that stops you from jumping in the car and going to the donut shop. If you have children you are trying to get off of junk - Sweet Treats will work very well. Even though these are sweet all of the recipes are loaded with fiber and are densely nutritious.

If all of this seems overwhelming, it is! That's why I suggest making the transition in a pace you can deal with. Rather than doing nothing, do what you can, then as time goes on take the next step. It took me four years before I had the courage to do the whole program. Let me tell you I feel great. If you fall off the wagon, don't be discouraged. Get right back on, it's a journey worth taking.

So you say, why is there even a section for sweet treats? Because we are human and will need to 'cheat' from time to time, and I would rather see you cheat with these healthful recipes than a box of commercial chocolates, cookies or an "over-the-counter" banana cream pie.

I can not stress becoming a label reader strongly enough. Even reading the labels may not be enough. The FDA does not require manufacturers to list items that have been used to process the listed ingredients. Examples of common items used that are not on the label are gluten, corn and soy. Unfortunately, most of the additives used in non-organic processed foods are man made chemicals good for shelf life only.

Sweets & Treats

Be equally aware of the words artificial or natural. Two examples of the word 'artificial' are Piperonal - extensively used as a substitute for vanilla, it is also used to kill lice, and Benzyl acetate - provides strawberry flavor and is used as a solvent for plastics. Artificial sweeteners are included in my list of dangerously unhealthy alternatives to processed sugar. When choosing oil, look for the words expeller pressed or cold pressed. If those words are not on the label assume a chemical or heat has been used to extract the oil. With the word natural on the label you assume the product is healthier for you, however, it does not mean it is something you are not allergic to (corn for example) or that it is truly healthy.

At this point let me say a word about stevia. Stevia is the leaf of an herb found in South America (the natives have been eating it for hundreds of years) and is the only sweetener I know of that does not allow Candida to grow. The FDA recently approved it for human consumption in the U. S. (they have also been eating it for years in Europe and the Orient). It is 300 times sweeter than sugar - a little goes a long way. I encourage you to find some and use it. It can usually be found in the herbal section of your local Health Food Store or at www.feelgoodfood.com.

Other healthier sweets are Agave Nectar and Xylitol. Both are low-glycemic, which means, the human body will not register the same highs and lows it does with high-glycemic sugars found (for example) in white potatoes, bananas, honey and refined sugar. The Xylitol may be used one for one to replace refined sugar but is non-fermenting in the body! For Agave Nectar, substitute 1/4 less than you would honey. Again, look for this product in your local health food store.

Treat your body with respect and it will serve you for a long time, a trim fit body is the by product of a healthy lifestyle. The first time a friend told me an overweight person is a malnourished person, I didn't have a clue as to what she was talking about. Then she said, "Don't believe me, start reading and see for yourself." I now make the same challenge to you. On to the 'Sweet Treats'. . .

Easy Treats

The kids want a treat and you want it easy. Does this sound familiar? You've had a long, hard day and someone near and dear to you is craving a treat. There are no premade frozen goodies in the freezer, you have had your one piece of fruit for the day and you want so desperately to be 'good'. Here are a few of the many, many possibilities. As time goes on you will be able to add to this list. For now. . . Crack a whole coconut, the kids love the milk and the fresh meat is heavenly — but make sure it is not moldy before drinking the milk.

Each shopping excursion buy a new exotic fruit to keep on hand in anticipation of a crave attack. Try a pomegranate, cactus pear, star fruit, kiwi or what ever strikes your fancy. Try something new, add to your food expertise! Chances are by the time you are through experimenting, the craving will have passed.

In ancient Rome, runners were sent to mountain tops by the elite to retrieve snow. Fresh squeezed fruit juice would then be poured over it for the first Italian Ice. An inexpensive ice shaver can be purchased for under $20. It will more than pay for itself with the amount of satisfaction it brings and will save you a run to a mountain top.

Don't let the ugly appearance of a jicama stop you from experiencing its mild flavor and delightful crunch. Peal and slice, add a squeeze of lime juice and a dash of sea salt and this root's inner beauty will shine.

Carrot juice with a hint of beet juice is unbelievably good. Frozen fresh carrot juice can be purchased at health food stores. Serve in a stemmed glass with a lemon wedge and a celery stalk.

Make a cocktail from 1/4 glass fruit juice (my favorite is pomegranate juice) and 3/4 glass sparkling water.

Toss a handful of nuts in a mix of vanilla, stevia and cinnamon and roast 10 minutes in a 350° oven.

Freeze fruit in small bites and retrieve for a refreshing, cool snack.

Change the focus, play a board game, read to each other, learn to weave. Stop food craving dead in its tracks by turning off the TV. No, I'm not crazy — it works! TV and late night, weekend snacking go hand in hand. Studies show that excessive TV watching physically slows your body metabolism.

Tapioca Pudding

This pudding can be as casual or as fancy as you wish, depending on the occasion. The visual presentation is the key. That, however, can be said about most food. If something looks appetizing, people will at least give it a try. The temperature at which it is served is also important. To chill or not to chill, that is the question! Nothing is worse than tepid soup or an ice cold sandwich. Served hot or cold, this is a wonderful treat.

5 Minutes to Prepare

5 Minutes to Cook

Over Night to Soak Tapioca

Small Pan / Stove Top / Spoon

Serves 2

VARIATIONS

- Turn into an elegant parfait. Layer with fresh berries or fruit in a long stemmed glass and serve chilled. If you do not have traditional parfait glasses, any stemmed glass can work – water, wine, even beer glasses.
- For crepe's, use Quinoa Pancakes, page 33. These can be made ahead and frozen until needed. If you make them fresh, cover crepes with an inverted bowl and allow them to sit a while until they cool and become more pliable. Fill with tapioca and fruit.
- Make a pie crust using the Very Berry Coffee Cake dough from pages 44-45 or Pear Tart Crust on pages 148-149. Bake, cool and fill with pudding, chill at least 3 hours. Top with fresh fruit and serve.

Ingredients

- 1/2 cup whole Tapioca Pearls
- 1 tablespoon Agar Agar flakes
- 1 cup Gluten-Free Brown Rice beverage,
  (Combine first three ingredients and soak over night in refrigerator)
- 1/2 teaspoon Sea Salt *(Necessary for taste)*
- 1 cup Gluten-Free Brown Rice beverage

- 1 heaping tablespoon Cashew Butter or
  Almond Butter or Sesame Tahini
- 1 teaspoon Vanilla
- 6 drops liquid Stevia or to taste
- Few grains of Cardamom *(Optional)*

- 1 cup Berries *(For variation only)*

PREPARATION

Combine first five ingredients in a sauce pan and simmer for 5 minutes or until tapioca becomes translucent. Remove from heat and add next four ingredients, stir with a spoon until all are evenly blended. Spoon into bowls and serve at once or assemble a variation and serve chilled.

SERVING SUGGESTION

Depending on the variation used, this is a very versatile recipe. Breakfast, lunch, dinner or midday snack.

Note: If using a non-alcohol vanilla increase amount to 1 tablespoon.

Almond Biscotti

Biscotti has always been near and dear to my heart — dunked into strong coffee and enjoyed while chatting with a friend. I still spend time with friends, except now it's this recipe and a cup of herb tea. If allergic to almond, use walnut and vanilla — the biscotti are still wonderful!
Remember, the companionship of friends and family is what is truly important, not the unhealthy cookie and coffee. When a person changes, people close to them may be afraid of loosing the closeness, please be understanding.

20 MINUTES TO PREPARE

45 MINUTES TO BAKE

OILED & FLOURED COOKIE SHEET

SAUCE PAN , BOWL, SPOON, KNIFE

OVEN TEMPERATURE 425° AND 350°

18 BISCOTTI

VARIATIONS

- Add 1/2 cup chopped dried cherries or other dried fruit. Different variety of nut or seed, or keep the batter plain.

- Use a baking stone for a crisper cookie.

- Grind nuts into flour before adding to recipe, press batter into a pie pan and bake. Fill with fresh fruit, yum.

- Drop by tablespoons and make almond cookies. You will only need to bake once.

-

- _____

Note: This recipe is not suitable for individuals allergic to tree nuts unless you omit or substitute nuts and extracts from made from nuts and oils.

Ingredients

- 2 cups Rice flour · GLUTEN-FREE
- 1/2 cup Tapioca flour
- 1 teaspoon Baking Soda
- 1/2 teaspoon Vitamin C Crystals
- 1/2 teaspoon Sea Salt

- 1 cup pure Water
- 2 teaspoons Agar Agar
- 1/2 cup Brown Rice Syrup
- 1/8 teaspoon Stevia
- 1 teaspoon Almond Extract
  or 1 tablespoon Almond Paste

- 1 cup Whole Almonds
- Flour and Oil for cookie sheet

PREPARATION

Mix together all dry ingredients. In a sauce pan, bring water and agar agar to a boil, turn down heat and simmer for 5 minutes. Remove from heat, add brown rice syrup (oiling the measuring cup first will keep the rice syrup from sticking). Add stevia and almond extract or paste. Stir until all is smooth and well combined. Pour all at once into dry ingredients and combine. Add almonds and mix one last time.

Generously oil and flour cookie sheet. Form an 18" by 4" rectangle down center of cookie sheet. Bake in a pre-heated 425° oven for 15 minutes; remove from oven and allow to cool. Cut 1" by 4 " strips. Arrange cut side down on a cookie sheet and return to a 350° oven for another 30 minutes or until golden.

Allow to cool before serving.

Note: This is not a suitable recipe as is if allergic to tree nuts.

Pineapple Lemon Pie

No one will ever guess how easy this tropical delight is to make. So yummy it will be hard to stop at one slice! This is a good recipe to try out on those people who never touch "health food." They will be asking for the recipe! This pie is a favorite to bring to pot-lucks and picnics!

20 Minutes to Prepare

Processor, Glass Pie Pan

Colander, Bowl, Spoon

Oven, Stove Top and Chill

Serves 8

VARIATIONS

- If soy is an option for you try this creamy topping. 1 -12.3 oz package Japanese style silken extra firm tofu - 1/4 cup coconut oil - 1/2 teaspoon stevia powder - 1 tablespoon vanilla - 2 tablespoons agave nectar - 1-1/2 cups dry soylait instant soy beverage. Place all in blender and process till smooth and creamy.

- Top with Creamy Frosting page 165 or Special Day Frosting page 166.

- _____

- _____

- _____

Ingredients

CRUST:

- 1 cup shelled Walnuts or puffed rice
- 1 cup Brown Rice flour ·GLUTEN-FREE
- 1/2 cup Tapioca Starch
- 1/2 teaspoon Sea Salt
- 2 tablespoons light Expeller Pressed oil or Coconut oil
- 2 tablespoons Maple Syrup or Honey or Agave Nectar
- 1/2 teaspoon Stevia Liquid Concentrate
- 1 small jar organic Pear baby food

FILLING:

- 1-20 oz. can crushed Pineapple in it's own juice - separated
- 1 cup shelled Walnuts (optional)
- Juice from one Lemon
- 2 tablespoons Agar Agar
- 1/2 teaspoon Stevia Liquid Concentrate or to taste

PREPARATION

Crust: Place all dry ingredients into processor and process until ground fine. Add baby food and all liquid ingredients and process until smooth. Press dough into an oiled and floured pie pan and form crust. Bake 350° for 20 minutes.

Filling: While crust is baking put together the filling. Using a colander, separate juice from pineapple, place juice in saucepan, reserve pineapple. Add lemon juice, agar agar and stevia to juice, bring to a boil and reduce heat and simmer five minutes. Place crushed pineapple, walnuts and hot liquid mixture in processor and combine just till nuts are chopped. Do not puree. Pour into prepared hot baked crust and chill.

SERVING SUGGESTIONS

This may also be made into thin squares just press crust into a 9"x13" cake pan and follow rest of the directions. Top with Creamy Frosting and whole strawberries and/or kiwi slices. Dress up or dress down. Enjoy!

Pear Tart

For over a year and a half my son was unable to eat apples and pears. Apples are still a no no, however; we have been able to reintroduce pears. In celebration of that event I concocted this sweet treat. Even I was surprised to discover how truly enjoyable it is. I love to watch people enjoy food I have prepared; (my husband says its because I'm Italian). Whatever the reason, this is one of those recipes where everyone wants seconds. It takes so little to make me happy!

30 MINUTES TO PREPARE

45 MINUTES TO BAKE

2 MIXING BOWLS, SPOON

CUTTING BOARD, KNIFE

10" ROUND BAKING DISH

OVEN TEMPERATURE 350°

8 TO 10 SLICES

VARIATIONS

• Use apples or blueberries instead of pears or combine all three.

• Make individual tarts using the bottoms of a cupcake tin.

• Substitute 1/4 cup ground hazel nuts for 1/4 cup amaranth, these nuts have a very distinctive taste and are worth a try.

• Bake the crust by itself and spread a half inch layer of Creamy Frosting page 165 on top. Dip sliced fruit in a solution of 2 cups water and 1/2 teaspoon vitamin C crystals, to keep from turning brown. Arrange on top do not re-bake.

•

•

Ingredients

- 3/4 cup Amaranth flour · GLUTEN-FREE
- 1/2 cup Pocono Cream of Buckwheat, uncooked
- 1/2 cup Arrowroot flour or 1/2 cup brown Rice flour
- 1 teaspoon Nutmeg
- 1/2 teaspoon Sea Salt
- 1/2 teaspoon Baking Soda
- 1/2 teaspoon Vitamin C crystals

- 1/4 cup Pear or Apple juice concentrate
- 1/8 teaspoon Stevia
- 1/4 cup Canola oil or Hazelnut oil

- 3 large ripe Pears

PREPARATION

Combine first seven ingredients, set aside. Combine next three and add to dry. Sprinkle some Cream of Buckwheat granules or rice flour in the bottom of a 10" quiche/tart/pie pan. Drop the dough by spoonfuls evenly around bottom of pan, with your fingers press together to evenly cover bottom of pan. Slice Pears in half lengthwise, core and slice halves into 1/4" slices. Arrange on top of crust. Bake at 350° for 45 minutes.

SERVING SUGGESTIONS

A nice fall treat to enjoy with a hot cup of green tea, an old movie or a good book. With all of the extra food preparation you do, you deserve it!

Plum Upside Down Cake

You know this is going to taste good before you dig in. Making food appealing to sight and smell is as important as taste. When baked in the bottom of a cake, plums become a rich luscious feast for the eye. This simple cake used to be a favorite after school treat at our house. When not using eggs or dairy products dryness can be a problem in baking. Fresh fruit adds the moistness needed, not to mention natural sweetness.

20 Minutes. to Prepare

40 Minutes. to Bake

One 8" or 9" Round Cake Pan

2 Bowls, Spoon

Knife, Cutting Board

Oven Temperature 375°

Oiled Wax Paper Cut to Fit Pan

6 – 8 Servings

VARIATIONS

- Instead of plums use apricot (dried sulfite-free will work if soaked in water ahead of time), peach, nectarine, sweet cherries, or the obvious pineapple. If you use pineapple, rings are nice with a sweet dark cherry in the centers of each ring and some chopped walnuts.
- Make individual cakes using a muffin tin. If you want to get fancy, serve in a pool of pureed fruit.
- Garnish with slivered almonds.
- Add 1/2 cup chopped, pitted, dried cherries to batter instead of fresh fruit and make cookies.
- _____
- _____

Ingredients

- 1 cup rolled Oats · GLUTEN or cooked Rice · GLUTEN-FREE, soaked for 15 minutes in 1/2 cup cold pure Water or Rice Beverage
- 2 tablespoons Raw Clover Honey or Agave Nectar
- 1/4 teaspoon liquid Stevia
- 1/3 cup Sesame or Canola oil

- 1-1/2 cups Oats · GLUTEN or Rice flour · GLUTEN-FREE
- 1 tablespoon Cinnamon
- 1/2 teaspoon Vitamin C Crystals
- 1/2 teaspoon Baking Soda
- 1/2 teaspoon Sea Salt

- 4 large ripe fresh organic Plums or 6 small, any variety

PREPARATION

Combine first four ingredients. Combine next five, then add liquid to dry. Gently mix with a spoon. Chop one of the plums, do not peel, and add to the batter and gently blend in. Cut unbleached wax paper to fit into bottom of pan, oil both sides, and place in bottom of pan. Cut remaining plums into 1/2 inch segments, discard stones, arrange segments in an attractive pattern on top of the oiled paper (remember these will become the top of the cake). Spoon batter evenly over fruit, it will be thick and sticky so be careful not to disturb fruit. Bake 40 minutes at 375°. Allow to cool 10 minutes. Place a plate on top and invert, remove wax paper, serve warm or at room temperature.

SERVING SUGGESTIONS

Snack, dessert, lunch box. Serve warm in a bowl with Rice Milk or Almond milk poured over the top.

Note: Do not use honey or agave nectar if on a strict Candida diet. Increase Stevia.

Carrot Muffins or Cake

Being a purist, I made this recipe for a year using a gluten grain, barley flour (all ingredients from day two of my rotation). It was OK but not the wonderful carrot cake I remembered! Then it hit me - use spelt (from day four) or gluten-free rice. What can I say ?

One year I placed the baked muffins in special Easter paper cups, decorated with little plastic bunnies in the tops and wrapped all in cellulose and ribbon. A chocolate bunny wouldn't have made my five year old happier.

FOOD PROCESSOR OR GRATER

BATTER 15 MINUTES TO PREPARE

2 MIXING BOWLS & SPOON TO COMBINE

60 - 65 MINUTES TO BAKE

OIL MUFFIN TINS/PAN, LIGHTLY FLOUR

OVEN TEMPERATURE 325°

8 REGULAR OR 24 MINI MUFFINS
OR A 8"x 8" CAKE PAN

VARIATIONS

- Any flour may be used, please see conversions page 185.
- If you cannot use pineapple, try a grated apple or pear in chunky applesauce or organic pear baby food to equal the amount of pineapple.
- If you wish, frost with any Cake Topper ideas pages 164-167. Garnish with pecans and carrot curls.
- This is a good recipe to make ahead and freeze. If you are going to freeze, do not defrost until just prior to serving.
-

Ingredients

- 1 cup packed grated Carrots
- 1 - 16 oz. can crushed Pineapple or fresh, with juice
- enough pure water (if needed) to bring Pineapple and juice to equal 2 cups
- 2 tablespoons Agave Nectar
- 1/4 cup Walnut oil or Olive oil
- 1/2 teaspoon Stevia (liquid)
- 1-1/2 teaspoon ground Cinnamon
- 2 cups Spelt flour · GLUTEN
  or 2 cups Rice flour · GLUTEN-FREE combined with 1/2 cup Tapioca flour
- 1/2 teaspoon Vitamin C Crystals
- 1 teaspoon Baking Soda
- 1 teaspoon Sea Salt
- 3/4 cup chopped Pecans (optional)

PREPARATION

Combine first seven ingredients. Mix the four dry ingredients together and add to the liquid previously prepared. Gently hand stir. If you wish, add the nuts at this point. Do not over stir. Spoon into a well oiled and floured cake pan or muffin tin. Bake for one hour at 325° or until tests done with toothpick.

SERVING SUGGESTIONS

Tasty lunch box treat. Serve to guests with a dollop of Creamy Frosting page 165 and pineapple chunks as garnish.

Note: Omit agave nectar if on a Candida diet and add extra Stevia to taste

Basic Carob Brownies

Easy to make, these delightful brownies are perfect to tuck into a purse, pocket or bag lunch. They freeze well and don't fall apart the way some non egg treats do when transported. They also look 'normal', normal that is, depending on your point of view. Carob is often used as a chocolate substitute, quite unfair to this naturally sweet and healthful little bean. I feel carob should be eaten for its own merits and not as a substitute for anything.

15 Minutes to Prepare

30 Minutes to Bake

2 Mixing Bowls, Spoon

Oil 8"x 8" Cake Pan, Lightly Flour

Oven Temperature 350°

16 Squares

VARIATIONS

- Check conversion chart on page 185 to make gluten-free.
- Cookies instead of squares. Drop by tablespoon fulls onto oiled cookie sheet, top each cookie with raw pecan half or sprinkle with flaked coconut. Bake at 350° for 12 minutes.
- Use brown rice syrup and stevia in place of honey - or - if on a strict candida diet use 1 cup brown rice milk with a heaping tablespoon of agar agar and 1/2 teaspoon stevia in place of honey.

- _____
- _____
- _____

Ingredients

- 2 cups Spelt flour · NON HYBRID WHEAT
- 1/2 cup finely ground Walnuts
  or Pecans or additional
  1/2 cup Spelt flour
- 1/2 cup Carob powder
- 1/2 teaspoon Sea Salt

- 1 cup Tupelo Honey or 3/4 cup Agave Nectar
- 1/2 cup Canola oil
- 1/4 cup pure Water

- 1/2 cup chopped Pecans or Walnuts (optional)
- 2 tablespoons. Tupelo Honey or Agave Nectar (optional)
- 16 Pecan or Walnut halves (optional)

PREPARATION

Combine first four ingredients. In separate bowl, blend next three. Pour liquid ingredients in with dry and stir just until evenly moistened, do not over mix. Fold in chopped nuts. The batter will be very thick. Spoon into a well oiled and floured 8"x8" cake pan. Place one nut half into what will be the center of each square, 4 across and 4 down. Bake 350° for 30 minutes. While still hot out of the oven brush tops with honey or agave nectar. When cool, cut into 16 squares. If you plan to freeze any portion, do so now.

SERVING SUGGESTIONS

Best when eaten with your fingers and a cup of hot mint tea.

Note: If candida overgrowth is a concern, use rice milk & agar agar in place of honey & sweeten with Stevia. See variations.

Carob Cake

I was tempted to name this the birthday cake, since that is usually when it is made - or should I say created. Since a butter cream frosting is probably not an option for you, decorating a cake for a special occasion can be challenging. May I suggest, when decorating for a child, trying Sorbie Lolli Pops stuck around sides or a favorite toy on top , one year I found train candle holders, page XI. For an adult occasion edible flowers are wonderful, nasturtium, bachelor buttons . . . Sparklers?

10 MINUTES TO PREPARE

30-35 MINUTES TO BAKE

2 MIXING BOWLS, SPOON

8" ROUND CAKE PAN

WAX PAPER

OVEN TEMPERATURE 350°

SERVES 12

VARIATIONS

- Frost with any of the frosting or pudding recipes. See pages 164-167.
- Cut cakes in half to make four layer cake. Alternate layers with Creamy Frosting made with pears pages 164-167 and fruit (cherries, bananas, peaches, strawberries, etc.).
- Mock German chocolate cake with Coconut Frosting, page 165.
- Black Forest cake with Coconut Pudding page 166 or Tapioca Pudding pages 142-143 and Cherries. Use 4 cups sweet dark cherries; organic fresh frozen are the best choice. Cut two cakes in half to make four layers. Divide pudding and cherries into four equal portions. Start with cake, then layer of pudding and cover with cherries, repeat three more times ending with cherries. Chill.

Ingredients

Note: double ingredients for a two layer cake

- 2 cups Spelt flour · NON HYBRID WHEAT
- 2/3 cup Carob powder
- 1 teaspoon Baking Soda
- 1/2 teaspoon Vitamin C Crystals
- 1/2 teaspoon Sea Salt

- 1/2 cup Tupelo Honey or
  Agave Nectar
- 1/2 cup Canola oil
- 3/4 cup pure Water

PREPARATION

Combine first five ingredients. Combine next three. Pour liquid ingredients into dry and hand mix just till evenly moist; do not over mix. Cut wax paper shaped to fit into the bottom of the cake pan(s), oil both sides and place into bottom of pan(s), flour. Pour batter into pan(s). Bake in a 350° oven for 30 minutes. Do not over bake - done when toothpick inserted in center comes out clean. Be sure to remove wax paper before decorating or serving.

SERVING SUGGESTIONS

This cake is flavorful and rich, not moist. To compensate for this slather with pudding, and or fruit. If you want the cake but you don't want the work, make a sheet cake, cut into squares and serve in a pool of Sweet Oat sauce 160-161. If you wish make the gluten-free variation on page 156.

Note: If on a candida diet, omit honey, replace with 1/4 cup water and use Stevia to taste.

Poached Pears

Similar to baked apples, yet somehow more elegant. Just the name poached, rather than baked, elevates this fruit to some higher standing. Served solo or grouped together in perfect harmony - always beautiful, always in good taste, literally! Look for large ripe fruit, with stems intact. While having nothing to do with flavor, the stems will add appeal to the final presentation. If you do lose a stem or two, replace with a small dried bay leaf or sprig of mint, you may wish to do this regardless.

5 MINUTES PER PEAR TO PREPARE

30 MINUTES TO POACH

MELON BALLER, VEGETABLE PEELER

15 TO 30 MINUTES. TO REDUCE LIQUID

NON REACTIVE POT (GLASS IS BEST)

ONE PEAR PER PERSON

VARIATIONS

- To add color to this dish, add a half cup beet to juice to pear juice. If you are serving these together you may want to do half of the pears white and the other half red.

- Serve pears in a nest of Cranberry Relish. . . One bag fresh cranberries, One small can frozen pineapple juice concentrate, stevia to taste. Combine all, add water to just cover cranberries. Bring to a boil, reduce heat and simmer ten minutes. Serve warm or chill to thicken. This is also very good served with holiday fare.

- Sprinkle tops with toasted chopped nuts or maple syrup or sugar.

- In a hurry? Instead of reducing liquid, use syrup on page 167.

- Place cinnamon stick or vanilla bean in poaching liquid.

- Garnish with a mint sprig or pansies or. . .your choice!

Ingredients

- One large ripe Pear per person
- Pear juice to just cover Pear/s
- chopped Nuts (optional)

PREPARATION

Pears will turn brown soon after contact with air so complete one pear at a time. Working quickly, wash and peal pear(s) leaving stems intact. Cut a thin slice off bottom, just enough to sit flat. Without disturbing outside appearance, working from bottom, scoop out lower seeded portion of core and discard, a small melon baller works best.

Place in a non-reactive pan with a lid just large enough to accommodate number of pears being prepared. Add correct amount of juice to just cover pears as you go. Bring to a boil, simmer with the lid on for 30 minutes or until tender not mushy. Using a slotted spoon, remove pears from liquid, place on serving dish. If any of the variations have been used, remove all foam and chunks from liquid and boil without lid until liquid is reduced to approximately 1/2 cup per pear. The amount of time will vary depending on amount of liquid started with. Pour liquid over pears, garnish. Serve warm or place in airtight container and chill up to 24 hours.

Be sure to poach pears in a sweet liquid. Plain water will leach all the flavor from the fruit.

SERVING SUGGESTIONS

A knife may be needed to cut into these, make sure your guests have access to one. These have a tendency to dry out, if you are going to serve them chilled, be sure keep the pears in liquid and air tight.

Note: Because of proper food combining fruit should be eaten raw first thing in the morning. Make this a once in awhile treat, served with a salad.

Sweet Oat Sauce

I found the idea for this recipe in a vegetarian magazine. With a few minor changes it fit right in with the way we eat. So many vegan recipes work well for those allergic to both eggs and dairy. The work involved with 'converting' conventional foods has been done for you. Be creative and this sauce/frosting can be used in so many ways. If on a gluten-free diet, use rice in place of oats.

5 Minutes to Put Together

2-5 Minutes to Puree

20 - 25 Minutes to Simmer - Spoon

Sauce Pan - Processor or Blender

5 Cups Sauce

VARIATIONS

- Convert sauce into a frosting. Thicken with 1/4 cup arrowroot, kudzu, agar agar, ground flax seeds, tapioca starch or carob during the last five minutes of simmering, puree, cool slightly and pour over cake or individual pieces, chill.
- Use another sweet juice in place of pineapple.
- Make gluten-free use white Basamati rice in place of oats.
- _____
- _____
- _____

Ingredients

- 1 cup rolled Oats · GLUTEN
  or Rice · GLUTEN-FREE
- 4 cups unsweetened Pineapple juice
- 1/4 cup Sesame Tahini

- 1-1/2 teaspoons Vanilla*
- 2 tablespoons Clover Honey or Agave Nectar
  or 1/4 teaspoon Stevia

PREPARATION

Combine first three ingredients in a saucepan, cover and bring to a boil. Lower heat and simmer 30 minutes. Remove from heat. Add remaining ingredients, puree in blender one cup at a time until smooth. Steam from hot liquids may cause top of blender to 'explode' off, to prevent this, hold lid up slightly to vent the steam when you first start to process.

SERVING SUGGESTIONS

Serve baked apples or poached pears sitting in a pool of this sauce. Cut brownies into diamond shapes, place on wire rack, use frosting variation with carob to pour over tops, chill, remove from rack and decorate with one perfect edible flower on top.

Note: Omit honey and use only stevia if on a candida diet.
*Note: If using non-alcohol vanilla, increase amount to 1 tablespoon.

Sorbet

The first summer was the worst. I had been prepared for just about anything, but not for the seductive siren song of the ice cream truck driving through our neighborhood three times a day, every day, all summer long. Children were eating their treats in front of my crying three year old. Words just do not work in some situations. This was one of those times and frozen fruit juice was a poor substitute for a Barney Pop. I soon discovered that fresh fruit sorbet can satisfy the worst ice cream craving.

KNIFE AND CUTTING BOARD

10 MINUTES TO PEEL AND DICE

CUTTING BOARD, KNIFE

5-10 MINUTES TO PROCESS

SEVERAL HOURS TO FREEZE

FOOD PROCESSOR

2 CUPS PER SERVING

VARIATIONS

- Substitute any fruit or melon, or combination of fruit (please review the food combining chart on page 25). Papaya's may need a tablespoon of honey or agave nectar or stevia and a squirt of lime juice.
- Watermelon is wonderful, however, beware it could cross react with ragweed, if you are allergic to pollen.
- Spoon into pop sickle forms and freeze.
- Puree fruit first and freeze in an ice cream maker.
- Pear sorbet is my favorite with fresh lemon zest and a squeeze of agave nectar!

Ingredients

- 2 cups cubed frozen fruit - choose one: Strawberry, Mango, Peach, Pineapple, Papaya, Pear, Melon or Banana work best.
- Sweeten using Agave Nectar, Raw Honey or Stevia to taste
- See variations and serving suggestions

PREPARATION

Select ripe yet firm organic fruit, wash well and peal. Remove pit or core. Cut into 1" chunks, place onto a cookie sheet and freeze an hour or two until frozen through. You may place chunks into a freezer safe container for use at a later time or prepare now.

Place one cup of fruit chunks into food processor and process until smooth, add remainder of frozen fruit one chunk at a time through hole in top of processor while running. Keep processing until texture becomes smooth. You will need to add a tablespoon of honey, agave nectar or some stevia to papaya and raspberries, adding sweetener to the other fruit will depend on its sweetness. . . Serve immediately.

SERVING SUGGESTIONS

Bananas become transformed into an ice cream like confection, that freezes well (for a short time).

Individual fruit plates with a scoop of pineapple sorbet is a wonderful summertime treat. Breakfast anyone?

Note: Do not use honey or agave nectar if on a candida diet, use stevia.

Cake Toppers

I use the term Cake Toppers instead of frosting because to say frosting would be misleading. Nothing will replicate the creamy peaks that come to mind with traditional butter cream frosting. Without the use of hydrogenated oils, dairy or soy smooth and fluffy is not going to happen. However, don't despair, instead of relying on tired old ingredients put your imagination to work. Quite often appearance is more important than the ingredient choices, like the

raspberries on the tart at left! Please, be sure to go over the list of ideas. Remember fat is out and taste is in!

SEE INDIVIDUAL RECIPES

TIME AND UTENSILS WILL VARY

COOKING METHODS WILL VARY

PORTION SIZES WILL VARY

IDEAS

- Make cake in a bunt or angel food cake pan and place a large decorative natural candle in center and decorate with fresh flowers.
- Just before serving decorate with fresh fruit - or - serve already sliced in a puddle of fresh fruit puree, or Sweet Oat Sauce pages 160-161.
- Cover cake with a paper doily or home made paper cutout and dust with Devan™ Sweet natural brown rice sweetener or cinnamon or carob or all three remove paper and serve. See example on page 156.
- Decorate top with raw nuts before baking and brush with honey while just out of the oven.
- Use gluten-free rice syrup as 'glue' for fruit, nuts, edible flowers, coconut or a natural candy, for a special Birthday.
- For a dark frosting add 1/2 cup carob and 1/4 cup pure water. A couple drops of beet juice will make pink, a few grains of spirulina will make green and carrot juice will make yellow, etc.

Ingredients

CREAMY FROSTING

- 2 cups Pineapple juice (do not use fresh)
- 3 tablespoons Agar Agar
- 1/2 cup Cashew or Almond Butter or Sesame Tahini
- 1/4 teaspoon Stevia or to taste

PREPARATION

In a small sauce pan bring the juice to a boil and add agar agar, simmer another 5 minutes stirring constantly. Allow to set. Once firm, place all ingredients in the bowl of the blender or food processor and combine until creamy. Any fruit juice or nut butter may be substituted. Excellent on Carrot Cake/Muffins pages 152-153.

COCONUT FROSTING

- 2 cups unsweetened, unsulfureted, shredded Coconut
- 1 cup raw Pecans or Walnuts
- 1/4 cup Raw Honey or Agave Nectar or 6-8 drops Stevia or to taste
- Coconut Milk

PREPARATION

Combine coconut and pecans or walnuts in a food processor and process until powdered. Add honey or stevia and blend, add coconut milk one tablespoon at a time until spreading consistency. This makes a great mock German Chocolate Cake. Use with Carob Cake, see pages 156-157.

Note: Do not use honey or agave nectar if on a candida diet, use stevia.

Ingredients

SPECIAL DAY FROSTING

- 2 cups Water from a pure source
- 4 tablespoons Agar-Agar
- 1/2 cup Agave Nectar
- 1 teaspoon Vanilla extract
- 1/2 cup softened organic Butter or non-hydrogenated butter substitute such as Spectrum™ or Earth Balance™ Spread (contains soy) - or use Spectrum™ non-hydrogenated shortening with 1/4 teaspoon sea salt

PREPARATION

Boil first 3 ingredients in a sauce pan for 5 minutes or until Agar flakes are dissolved. Add Vanilla and pour into a glass cake pan and cool till firm. Cut into one inch squares and place into processor and process until creamy. Add butter or spread or shortening and continue to process until desired consistency is reached. Chill and use as you would Butter Cream frosting.

COCONUT PUDDING / FROSTING

- 1 - 14 oz. can Coconut Milk
- 2 tablespoons Kudzu
- 1/3 cup Maple Syrup or Honey or Agave Nectar
- 1/8 teaspoon Vitamin C Crystals or Lemon juice

PREPARATION

Combine all ingredients in a sauce pan. Whisk until all lumps are removed. Stirring constantly, heat until thick and bubbly. Cool and "whip" with an electric mixer, use between layers of a cake and/or on top as decoration. This may also be used to make coconut or banana cream pie, see Pie Crusts pages 167-173.

Ingredients

The following recipe contains butter if you are sensitive to dairy either avoid or use Spectrum™ or Earth Balance Spread™ (spreads contain soy). In moderation, this is wonderful. This 'syrup' was passed on to me by a friend/nutritionist, it is safe if you are on a candida diet and the taste. . . judge for yourself.

CANDIDA SAFE SYRUP

- 1 tablespoon organic unsalted Butter or Ghee or Spectrum Spread™ , Earth Balance Spread™
- 1 teaspoon Vanilla (non-alcohol is best)
- 6 drops liquid Stevia or to taste
- pinch ground Cinnamon
- pinch Sea Salt

PREPARATION

Just heat butter, ghee or spread (will not melt, mix cold) till melted in a sauce pan. Do not use margarine or anything hydrogenated. Turn off heat and add remaining ingredients. Once combined, pour over pancakes, waffles, cake or oat meal. Toss with a couple cups of raw walnuts or pecans and toast in a 350° oven for 10 minutes. Once cool, a hand full of these can satisfy a sweet snack craving. To store nuts spread out onto a cookie sheet and freeze, once frozen place in an air tight glass container to store frozen for enjoying another time.

SERVING SUGGESTIONS

Be creative with how you present these Cake Toppers. Perhaps a spoonful on top of an already cut piece of cake with a mint sprig or setting the cake on top is the way to go. An appetizing dessert is important to its acceptance by others. A pancake or waffle make an excellent sweet treat if presented properly.

Note: If using non-alcohol vanilla, increase amount to 1 tablespoon.

Pie Crust

Sometimes nothing will replace the heartwarming feeling that a pie can bring. Images of a crisp autumn day, Mom's hot apple pie cooling on the window-sill, the anticipation is as delicious as the pie itself. Most of the following recipe's are pretty straightforward. My son's favorite is the oat crust with a tart cherry filling. When he was little I made a cherry pie to bring along on vacations, he never feels left out and we all had a better time!

ROLLING PIN
WAX PAPER OR PASTRY CLOTH
10 MINUTES TO PREPARE
30-35 MINUTES TO BAKE SINGLE CRUST
PIE PLATE OR TART PAN
OVEN TEMPERATURE 350°
2 SINGLE OR 1 DOUBLE CRUST

VARIATIONS

- My Grandmother Page lived her entire life on a farm. She used to bake a flat pie crust on a cookie sheet. While still warm, she would break the crust up into the bottom of a bowl add some fresh fruit salad, more crust and top with more fruit salad. It has always amazed me how something so simple could taste so wonderful. Try it and I think you will agree.

- Bake in a tart pan, cool and fill with Creamy Frosting page 165. Top with fresh fruit and/or berries or press the pie dough up the sides of lightly oiled muffin cups and bake, for individual tarts.

- Make a fresh fruit pizza using a pizza pan or a quiche dish - or - fill with veggies and make a hearty chicken pot pie.

- Add stevia for a sweet crust.

- _____

Ingredients

QUINOA - GLUTEN-FREE

- 1 cup Quinoa flour
- 1/2 cup Tapioca starch
- 1/2 cup finely ground raw Cashew or Macadamia nuts. . . If you choose not to use nuts, substitute an additional 1/2 cup Quinoa.
- 1 teaspoon Nutmeg
- 1/2 teaspoon Sea Salt
- 1/3 cup Sunflower oil
- 1/4 cup pure Water

OAT - GLUTEN OR RICE - GLUTEN-FREE

- 3 cups Oat or Rice flour
- 1 tablespoon Agar Agar
- 1/2 teaspoon Sea Salt
- 1/2 cup Sesame oil
- 1 teaspoon Vanilla extract
- Add enough pure Water to Vanilla to equal 1/4 cup

AMARANTH - GLUTEN-FREE

- 2 cups Amaranth flour
- 1/2 cup Arrowroot starch
- 1/2 cup finely ground raw Hazelnut (Filbert)
- 1/2 teaspoon Sea Salt
- 1/3 cup Canola oil
- 1/4 cup pure Water

*Note: If using non-alcohol vanilla, increase amount to 1 tablespoon.

Ingredients

SPELT OR KAMUT - NON HYBRID WHEAT

- 2-1/4 cups Spelt or Kamut flour
- 1/2 teaspoon Sea Salt
- 1/2 cup light Olive oil
- 1/4 cup pure Water

MACAROON DOUGH

- GLUTEN-FREE

- 2 cups finely shredded unsulfureted and unsweetened Coconut
- 1 cup finely ground raw Walnuts or Pecans (optional)
- 1/2 cup Spelt or Rice flour
- 1 teaspoon fresh Orange zest
  (please, make sure the orange is organic, if not, do not use - Optional)
- 1/4 cup Walnut oil or Olive oil
- 2 tablespoons raw unprocessed Tupelo Honey or Agave Nectar
  or 1/4 teaspoon liquid Stevia to taste
- 1/3 cup pure Water or Coconut or Rice Milk

MOCK GRAHAM CRACKER CRUST - NON HYBRID WHEAT

- 1-1/4 cups Spelt flour
- 1-1/4 cups finely ground raw Pecans
- 1/2 teaspoon Sea Salt
- 1/3 cup pure Maple syrup or Candida Safe Syrup page 167
- 1/3 cup Walnut oil

Ingredients

CAROB CRUST - GLUTEN-FREE

- 1 cup Teff flour
- 1 cup Carob powder
- 1/2 cup finely ground raw Walnuts (optional)
- 1 tablespoon Coffee substitute (optional, may contain gluten grains or soy)
- 1/3 cup raw unprocessed Honey or Agave Nectar or pure Water & 1/2 teaspoon Stevia powder
- 1/3 cup light Olive or Walnut oil

SPICY CRUST

- 1-1/4 cup Chick Pea flour · GLUTEN-FREE
- 1-1/4 cup Kamut flour · NON HYBRID WHEAT
- 1/2 teaspoon each Garlic powder, Cumin, Onion powder, Oregano and Sea Salt
- 1/2 cup extra virgin Olive oil
- 1/4 cup pure Water or organic Vegetable Juice (may contain tomatoes)

Note: Omit all sweeteners except Stevia if on a candida diet.

Combine all dry ingredients in a large bowl. With pastry cutter or working with two knives cut oil evenly into the dry ingredients. Mixture should resemble coarse crumbs. Next combine all of the remaining liquid ingredients and slowly add to the mixture in the bowl. Continue to work with pastry cutter, you do not want to overwork the dough. If more liquid is needed at this point add water one teaspoon at a time until desired consistency is reached. Press into a ball.

The dough should hold together to form a ball and be able to hold its shape when pinched. Divide into two equal balls. One may be frozen in a freezer safe container for use at another time.

For the Macaroon, Graham Cracker, Carob and Spicy Crust, skip the following step, these crusts can be pressed directly into the pan and you may do so at this point. This type of dough unfortunately will not work as a double crust pie. However, if you like, a portion of the dough may be flattened and baked on a cookie sheet and then the remainder crumbled on top of the pie once filled.

Next, if working with the Quinoa, Oat, Rice, Amaranth, Spelt or Kamut, turn the dough out onto a well floured pastry cloth or an unbleached sheet of wax paper. Flatten as much by hand as possible keeping dough round and flat. With a floured rolling pin, roll dough to desired size, allow enough to roll and crimp for a decorative edge to pie. The next step is tricky, since some of these flours will not 'act' like wheat. Very carefully center pie pan upside down on top of dough. With one hand under wax paper and one hand on bottom of pie plate, invert. Gently press dough into pan and peel off cloth or paper. Make any repairs necessary in crust, and prick bottom with fork in several places.

With knife or scissors evenly cut dough hanging over edge (one inch is good), allowing enough to roll under to form a neat edge. If making a double crust pie, roll out second lump of dough large enough to fit on top. Fill first crust with desired filling and place second crust on top, peel off cloth or paper, cut top edges to match bottom crust. Gently roll dough under to make a neat edge, prick top with fork or make slits in top for steam to escape.

To make the fluted edge for either single or double crust, once edge has been rolled under, place first and second fingers behind dough gently press a thumb print in between fingers from other side, repeat this step until entire edge is fluted.

For single crust, bake in a 350° oven for 20 to 25 minutes or until lightly brown. If edges are browning too quickly, cover edges only with foil and continue baking.*

For double crust, bake in a 350° oven for 60 to 65 minutes or until center is bubbling and crust is golden. Halfway through baking, check edges. If browning too quickly, cover edges only with foil.*

Pies may be frozen before or after cooking. Allow more baking time if pie is frozen.

SERVING SUGGESTIONS

For the filling, use your favorite fruit pie recipe sweetened with stevia, agave nectar or xylitol tossed with a couple of tablespoons of tapioca flour.

Use a spring form pan, press Macaroon, Graham Cracker or Carob dough on bottom bake and cool. Fill with fruit and an agar agar and fruit juice gelatin. An absolutely beautiful example is Blood Orange juice, (the juice is naturally red), 'boost' the sweetness with stevia, pour over pineapple and banana chunks, chill. This is a summertime show stopper!

*Note: I do not recommend using aluminum foil to store or cook food. However, it is the easiest and most economical way to keep the crust edges from burning.

Sesame Candy

Whole sesame seeds are an excellent source of calcium. Believe it or not your body actually utilizes more of the calcium found in sesame seeds (or a half cup of broccoli for that matter) than it can utilize from dairy products. "This can't be", you say. . . "milk does a body good". You don't need to take my word for it; read for yourself. Studies done over the years have shown the human body's absorption of calcium may be blocked by high protein consumption. Have you read a milk carton lately?

10 MINUTES TO PREPARE / 24 HOURS TO REST

35 MINUTES TO BAKE

9" X 9" BAKING DISH/SMALL SAUCE PAN OVEN

TEMPERATURE 350°

MAKES A DOZEN 1" BY 2" CANDIES

VARIATIONS

- Use chopped nuts or coconut in place of sesame seeds.
- Replace honey with brown rice syrup, maple syrup or stevia, or use only stevia and non-alcohol vanilla if on a strict candida diet.

- _____

- _____

- _____

Ingredients

- 2 tablespoons raw unpasteurized Honey or Black Seed Honey Booster or Agave Nectar plus enough pure Water to equal one cup
- 1 heaping tablespoon Agar Agar
- 1/8 teaspoon liquid Stevia or to taste

- 1 cup raw hulled Sesame seeds

PREPARATION

Combine first three ingredients in a small sauce pan. Bring to a boil, reduce heat and simmer 5 minutes. Remove from heat and taste for sweetness, add more stevia one drop at a time, NOT honey, if not sweet enough. Add sesame seeds and mix thoroughly.

Spoon into 9" x 9" glass baking dish and press flat and smooth. Bake in a 350° preheated oven for 30 minutes or until golden. Allow to cool 24 hours and slice into desired sizes and shapes. Loosen from edges and remove with a spatula. These will crisp with time.

SERVING SUGGESTIONS

These make great cake decorations whole or crumbled. When crumbled, this candy is a nutritious topping for cake, pudding, pancakes or anything you can think of!

These are also healthy additions to your child's lunch.

Note: Honey is not suitable if on a strict candida diet.

Sugar is an Addiction

I don't believe that all messages coming through our brain are representative of who we truly are. The brain is the control center, the computer for our body. It is constantly receiving messages from every organ and cell. Including messages from organisms sharing space with us, such as microscopic parasites such as Candida Albicans. If you have ever seen living human blood under a microscope you know what I mean. A dirty internal environment invites these parasites to set up housekeeping. Once colonized they now have a say as to the type of foods we eat.

Since our brain needs sugar to operate and the parasites need sugar to proliferate, this is a match not made in heaven, but a match none the less. Small meals consisting of complex carbohydrates and quality proteins feed our brain in an efficient manner, keeping us awake and having energy during the day and allowing us to sleep at night. However, like a kid in a candy store, the brain will take all the sugar we can feed it. We will experience a rush of energy and a momentary high from the drug known as processed sugar. This feeling will be short lived since the brain is not set up to store the excess sugar. This excess sugar will be stored as fat in body tissue and as food for the unwanted parasites (who are always asking the brain for more). It will ferment and like alcohol it will affect our behavior. This is when we experience fatigue, headaches, depression and low energy. Like the monster in **Little Shop of Horrors** our brain starts chanting; feed me!

After a while we become addicted to the euphoric sugar high. In an attempt to stay awake or feel alive we look to more sugar. This sugar can be in the form of pasta, dairy products, cookies or fruit juice (all acid-forming). For the truly addicted there is the morning carbonated cola beverage and sweet roll or breakfast bar (all highly acid-forming). Because all of these foods and beverages are legal it does not occur to us the damage that is being done. After a while our body can no longer keep up with the type of clean-up that must be done just to maintain basic body functions. Soon the liver and the pancreas can't keep up. The first symptoms might be bad skin or acid reflux and heart burn. For some it is overweight and insomnia.

As with any addiction, recognizing we have a problem is the first step to recovery. Refined sugar is the gateway drug of choice for most of America. If you have ever gone cold-turkey with sugar you know what I am talking about. The craving can become almost unbearable. I have found that if you can go three days with no sugar, a big part of the battle is won. Basic rule: if it is wrapped in cellophane, comes out of a vending machine or contained in an aluminum can... don't eat or drink it. Just say no! ■

Resources

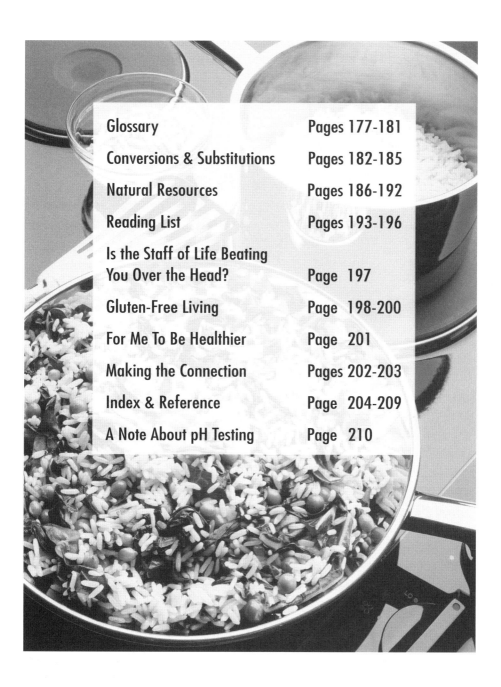

Glossary

Agar-Agar: (Kanten) a sea vegetable which can replace traditional animal based gelatin. Agar Agar does not need refrigeration to set.

Agave Nectar: (pronounced Ah-gav-eh) Neutral flavor. Usually organic, sweet cactus nectar extracted from the pineapple-shaped core of the Blue Agave. A 93% fruit sugar content, allows agave nectar to absorb slowly into the body, decreasing the highs and lows associated with sugar intake. Use 25% less in most recipes.

Amaranth: Ancient grain eaten by the Aztec, a complete vegetable grain protein. May be eaten whole or as a flour.

Arame: Sea vegetable with a mild sweet taste and texture, similar to mung bean threads.

Arrowroot: Used as a thickener for sauces and with non-gluten grains.

Asafetida: East Indian spice similar to garlic and onion when cooked. Look for pure asafetida, some may contain wheat.

Basmati Rice: Short grain pleasant tasting white and brown rice.

Bean Threads: Used in Oriental cooking, similar to angel hair pasta, made entirely from mung beans. Some brands may contain potato starch.

Bee Pollen: Rich source of nutrients collected from the pollen of plants.

Bragg Liquid Aminos™: Is a certified non-GMO liquid protein concentrate derived from soybeans containing 16 essential and non-essential amino acids in naturally occurring amounts. Wheat and gluten-free.

Brown Rice: Unprocessed whole grain rice with the outer germ intact, unlike white rice a complex carbohydrate.

Buckwheat: Technically a fruit, not related to wheat. Roasted groats make a hearty casserole, suitable as a main course, earthy flavor.

Buckwheat Soba: Oriental pasta made from Buckwheat. Often mixed with wheat make sure you are getting 100% Buckwheat Soba.

Chapati: East Indian flat bread. Yeast free.

Coconut Oil: A healthy fat that helps speed metabolism. Excellent choice for cooking because of its high smoke temperature.

Coffee Substitute: Usually made from roasted barley a gluten grain or soy. Read the label to find the brand best suited to your needs. Great way to quit caffeine.

Dasheen: Large tuber also known as taro and malanga.

Distilled Water: Water with minerals and chemicals removed, purest form of water.

Dulse: Sea vegetable, red salty sweet, good raw or cooked.

Expeller Pressed: Sometimes referred to as Cold Pressed. A process of extracting the oil without the use of heat, toxic chemicals, solvents or preservatives. Never allow oil to smoke, once this happens the healthful properties are lost.

Filbert: Small, young, Hazel nuts.

Flax: Oil from the seed is one of the highest vegetable source of Omega 3, an Essential Fatty Acid, necessary for healthy cells, always keep refrigerated. Flax is versatile, the plant is used to make linen and when heated, the oil makes linseed oil used as a furniture finish. The seeds may be eaten whole and make a great snack.

Ghee: Clarified butter, unsalted, lactose and casein free tolerated by some otherwise sensitive to dairy. Look for it in your local Health Food Store.

Gummies: A whole food supplement made from a blend of fruits and veggies in a gelatin base. Healthy candy that kids love. Order www.feelgoodfood.com-LINKS.

Hijiki: Sea Vegetable, choose black with no brown strands.

Hummus: A middle eastern dish made from ground chick peas (garbanzo beans). Great used as a spread or dip with Chapati.

Jicama: South American tuber, good raw or cooked. Peel and eat sliced thin, clean tasting with a great crunch, eat with lime juice and sea salt.

Kamut: Ancient Egyptian grain eaten by Cleopatra (or so they say). Like spelt, a non-hybrid wheat tolerated by some people who cannot eat modern age wheat. Avoid if on a gluten-free diet.

Kelp: Sea vegetable, good source of iodine and calcium. Good mixed with sea salt.

Kombu: Sea vegetable, dark brown deep sea kelp. A flavor enhancer, good for tenderizing beans and tough root vegetables. Excellent in soup stock.

Kudzu: Also spelled Kuzu. A root starch, thickens sauces, gravy & puddings.

Laundry Ball: One for the wash designed to safely 'beat' the clothes clean. With a laundry ball only a teaspoon of biodegradable soap is needed. A second set of laundry balls designed to fluff in the dryer making the need for fabric softener (an extremely allergenic and toxic substance) obsolete.

Miso: Contains fermented soy, sometimes mixed with brown rice or barley. Best known for soup stock but also good in dips, sauces and dressings.

Mochi: Made from brown rice that has been steamed and pounded. When grilled, it puffs up and becomes crunchy. Excellent toasted in a waffle iron.

Nigella Seed: Also known as Black Cumin even though not related. This herb has been used for millenniums to strengthen the immune system, cleanse the body and purify the blood. Typically used in Middle Eastern Breads.

Glossary

Non-Irradiated: A safe process of drying herbs without the use of radiation.

Nori: Sea vegetable usually processed in sheets. Commonly used as the wrapper for sushi and rice balls. Sweet and delicate, may also be toasted and crumbled over vegetables or rice.

Organic: Growers/packers of fruits, vegetables, meats and grains adhere to strict farming standards set by the government to insure the consumer minimal chemicals have been used at any stage of the product's life. Not only are these products good for you and agricultural workers, but they are good for Mother Nature and her ecosystem.

Pau d'Arco: The inner bark of a tree used as a tea. Excellent for controlling the growth of candida. Fungus will not grow on or around this tree. Start with a half cup of tea a day and work your way slowly up to a quart. May be sweetened with stevia.

Phytochemicals: The essential nutrients found in all vegetables.

Propolis: Made by bees to seal their honeycombs. Excellent immune booster.

Quinoa: (Keen-wah) Ancient grain eaten by the Incas. Supplies all the essential amino acids in a balanced pattern, often referred to as a super food. Use whole or as a flour. Whole grain works in place of rice and couscous. Be sure to wash grain before cooking to remove natural bitter coating.

Rice Milk: Milk alternative made from organic Brown Rice. Some rice brands are not gluten-free. Be sure to call the manufacturer first.

Rice Sticks: Oriental pasta made from 100% rice flour.

Royal Jelly: Fed to the Queen Bee by the worker bees. Contains 12-15% protein, 10-15% sugars, 3-6% fats a high concentration of vitamins, minerals, enzymes and amino acids along with antibacterial and antibiotic components.

Sea Salt: Saltier, so you use less. When iodine is added to salt so is sugar. (Keeps the salt from clumping.) If you need iodine, eat kelp. Sea Salt is not altered with chemicals or pollutants and contains a full complement of beneficial trace minerals.

Sourdough: A fermentation process done to a grain starter culture, it allows breads to rise without yeast. However, it is not a good idea to eat sourdough with a candida overgrowth.

Soy Milk: Milk alternative made from soy beans. Not all brands are gluten-free. Be sure to call the manufacturer.

Spectrum Spread: Organic non-hydrogenated margarine substitute made from canola oil, does contain soy. **Earth Balance Spread** is another margarine substitute.

Spelt: Ancient grain from Europe over 9,000 years old! A non-hybrid wheat, may be tolerated by many wheat sensitive people. Higher in gluten than wheat, excellent in baked goods and as a pasta. Avoid if on a gluten-free diet.

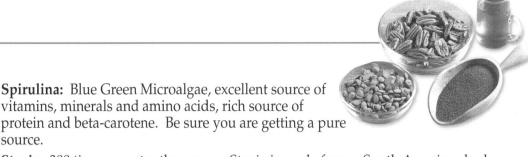

Spirulina: Blue Green Microalgae, excellent source of vitamins, minerals and amino acids, rich source of protein and beta-carotene. Be sure you are getting a pure source.

Stevia: 300 times sweeter than sugar. Stevia is made from a South American herb stevia rebaudiana. May be used in its powder form or as a liquid. This is the only sweetener I know of that does not allow candida to grow. A food grade medicinal herb, may help control blood sugar.

Sucanat: Dried juice from **SU**gar **CA**ne **NAT**ural.

Tahini: Paste made from sesame seeds, used to make Hummus.

Tamari: Soy sauce may be found wheat & MSG free, fermented.

Tapioca Starch/Flour: Use as you would corn starch, usually necessary with non-gluten flours.

Teff: From Ethiopia, the world's smallest grain. 150 grains of Teff equals the weight of one grain of wheat.

Umeboshi Plums: Pickled plums, soaked in brine with shiso leaves. These small red plums are excellent for digestion, helping to neutralize a high acid condition. Use the paste as you would mustard.

Unsulfated: Tells the consumer that a natural, safe drying process has been used without the use of sulfates as drying, preserving and bleaching agent.

Vanilla, Non-Alcohol: Contains glycerine instead of alcohol. There is no bitter aftertaste, only the sweet taste of vanilla, worth looking for! Alcohol based vanilla extract also contains gluten. Non-alcohol extracts are usually gluten-free.

VidaCell: Rice based polysaccharide peptide, functional food that helps to fight the cellular aging process providing essential nutrients to protect, repair and renew the body at the cellular level. www.feelgoodfood.com choose LINKS.

Vitamin C Crystals: Used by grandma in canning. Vitamin C in this form keeps the fruit from turning brown. When mixed with Baking Soda, a chemical reaction occurs, as with baking powder, allowing baked goods to rise.

Wakame: Sea vegetable, primarily used in miso soup, it can also be crumbled on top of vegetables as a tasty condiment.

Xanthan Gum: A common substitute for gluten, acts as a stabilizer, emulsifier and suspension agent to help dough rise well. Excellent in wheat-free baked goods.

Xylitol: Clinically proven to reduce cavities, low-glycemic and non-fermentable use as you would sugar. Can be found at: www.feelgoodfood.com

Conversions & Substitutions

Helpful Tip: Never be afraid or shy about asking for what you need or must have when in a restaurant. If you are polite, sincere and firm, 99 out of 100 times they will have something that will work for you, within reason. . . Never eat fast food! Learn to pack a lunch. Become an avid label reader. Listen to your body, no one lives in it but you!

BLACK PEPPER: I have found the following ingredients will lend a hot peppery taste to foods: ginger, watercress, radish, mustard seed, raw onion and garlic, extra virgin olive oil, horseradish and wasabi.

BREAD: Almost all have either sourdough or yeast cultures, avoid if Candida is a problem. Check out our Natural Resources section pages 186-192.

BUTTER: Spectrum Spread or Earth Balance Spread (contains soy). Please, never use margarine - it is too unhealthy. Almond butter, pistachio butter, macadamia butter, sesame tahini, hummus, sunflower butter, cashew butter, olive oil, herbed oil or a mashed avocado.

CHEESE: Read all labels most cheese substitutes contain casein and or soy. The Uncheese Cookbook by Joanne Stepaniak, almost all of her recipes contain nutritional yeast, but are quite good. For a swiss flavor try a mashed avocado, 2 tablespoons tahini and a squeeze of lemon.

CHOCOLATE: The most used chocolate substitute is carob. It looks and bakes like chocolate: however, the taste is different. When using carob, only a small amount of sweetener is needed, since it is naturally sweet and has a good flavor of its own. **Try This Sugar and Dairy Free Recipe for a substitute Chocolate Milk shake:** Start with one cup rice or almond milk beverage, plain. Add two heaping tablespoons carob, one teaspoon vanilla, one tablespoon almond butter, one fourth teaspoon stevia or to taste. Mix with ice in blender or heat for hot chocolate substitute. If you have an ice cream maker, this recipe makes great ice cream, or freeze as mock fudgesicles!

COFFEE: There are many coffee substitutes on the market that taste remarkably like coffee. Their main ingredient is usually roasted barley or soy. Some brand names are Cafix, Kaffree Roma, Pero, Sundance Grain Beverage and Yannoh (an organic substitute) and Teeccino.

CRACKERS: Rice Crackers, WASA Light Rye Krisp.

EGG: 1 egg = 1/3 cup water + 1 tablespoon ground flaxseed. Most recipes work with the addition of the ground seeds and an additional 1/3 cup liquid. Use as you would an egg for pancakes and baked goods. Multiply recipe for egg accordingly.

OTHER IDEAS: Applesauce, mashed banana or pumpkin, etc., one half cup per egg. There are also other fruit based egg replacers on the market specifically for this purpose or Egg Replacer, a commercial egg replacement by ENER - G Foods, Inc.

FRUIT & VEGETABLE GUMMIES: A unique treat, order from www.feelgoodfood.com choose LINKS from top bar.

GARLIC: An East Indian spice known as asafetida. May contain wheat, read label.

GELATIN: Many forms of gelatin come from animal sources. Vegetable gelatin works just as well and does not need refrigeration to set. Try agar agar (a sea vegetable) or kuzu (the root of a plant), Both found in the Macrobiotic section of your local health food store.

HERBS: Never consume irradiated herbs and spices, non-irradiated brands are available in health food stores, if the label does not state non-irradiated, it probably has been. Anything dried harbors mold, eat fresh whenever possible. Any sunny window-sill (or growlight) can make an attractive herb garden. All you need are containers, soil, seeds and water.

ICE CREAM: Pureed frozen fruit (see page 162-163), shaved ice with fresh fruit juice, frozen fruit juice, Rice Dream Frozen Desserts, Fruit Sorbet, Frozen Amazake, Farm Foods Frozen Ice Bean and Tofu Frozen Treats. Check your health food store. Read ALL labels.

LEAVENING: 1/2 Teaspoon Baking Soda + 1/2 Teaspoon Vitamin C Crystals = 1 Teaspoon Baking Powder. When combined with an egg replacement a very nice effect is achieved. Some commercial brands to try, Ener-G Foods Baking Powder, Rumford Baking Powder and Featherweight Baking Powder. Read labels.

LETTUCE: Sprouts, all types, both bean and seed, are an excellent crunchy substitution! Also try spinach, celery, cucumber, watercress or sweet pea pods.

MAPLE SYRUP: Candida Safe Syrup page 167.

Conversions & Substitutions

MILK: Nut milk, using a blender. Soak 1 cup raw nuts for 8 hours. Combine soaked nuts with 6 cups pure water, blend a minute or two on highest setting. Almonds may be blanched, add soaked almonds to boiled water for 30 seconds, drain and "pop" out of skin before blending. Strain through a new nylon stocking. Pulp may be used as flour or as "cheese" on top of a salad. Makes 2 quarts 'milk' use in recipes as you would milk. Stays good in refrigerator for 3 days. Packaged substitutions include, soy milk, rice milk, almond milk, coconut milk, and oat milk. Milk can be made from any nut, seed, bean or grain, the method is the same; soak, blend with water, strain.

MUSTARD: Umeboshi Plum Paste.

ONION: Nothing is ever going to taste just like an onion, however, you can fool your mouth with a similar crunch. Try the spine of a romaine lettuce leaf (raw only) slice thin across the grain and use as you would an onion or bok choy or celery, (may be cooked), and combined with watercress or radish. In cooked dishes, try asafetida, an East Indian spice.

PEANUT BUTTER: Other nut and seed butters, almond, cashew, pistachio, macadamia, sesame tahini and sunflower butters.

POTATO: Mashed or twice baked, try parsnips, cauliflower or great northern beans. Chip substitute - Terra Chips, Rice Bites, or Sweet Potato Chips. French Fry substitute - use jicama or jerusalem artichokes, slice and fry.

PROCESSED SUGAR: Stevia, agave nectar, xylitol, raw honey, maple syrup or raw sugar cane, sucanat or turbinado, date sugar, rice or barley syrup, Devansoy brown rice sugar, fruit juice or concentrate or whole fruit. If using liquid sweetener omit other liquids in recipe. If you suffer from a candida overgrowth, no amount of sugar is acceptable in any form except the herb stevia.

SALAD DRESSING: You have four options when dining out. (1) Eating what they have to offer and becoming ill, (2) Eating your salad dry, (3) Carrying your own 'safe' dressing pages 96-101 or (4) Ask for Oil and Lemon on the side.

SALT: Sea Salt, Real Salt, Spike Seasoning, Vege-Sal, Dr. Bronner's Seasoned Salt, etc. or make your own with kelp, sesame seeds, fennel seeds and anything you think might add spice to your food. Read all labels.

SOY SAUCE: Bragg Liquid Aminos - made from soy but contains no wheat and is not fermented, if you are not allergic to soy this is a better choice.

STARCH: Tapioca flour, arrowroot starch, jicama starch, dried bean flakes.

TEA: Replace with herba mate or herb tea. Also try: 1 teaspoon fennel or anise seed or 2 bay leaves or wintergreen or fresh mint leaves. To prepare pour a cup of boiling water over chosen ingredient and steep 5 to 15 minutes. Try Pau d' Arco to help with candida overgrowth. Shop for tea www.feelgoodfood.com.

TOMATO SAUCE: No Tomato Marinara, pages 122-123.

VANILLA: Spicery Shoppe Non-Alcohol Vanilla. Less is more, you won't believe how much better this tastes! Far more suitable for children. Experiment with another flavor peppermint, orange or almond for example.

VINEGAR: Lemon juice. Umeboshi Plum paste.

WHEAT FLOUR: 1 cup of wheat =

1 cup Spelt	3/4 cup Quinoa*	1 cup Rice*
1 cup Kamut	3/4 cup Amaranth*	1-1/3 cups Oats*
1 cup Teff	3/4 cup Buckwheat*	1-1/3 cups Barley*
	3/4 cup Chick Pea Flour*	1-1/4 cups Rye*

* For these grains, add 1/2 cup Tapioca or Arrowroot Starch.

Note: If you wish, the addition of Xanthan Gum or Agar Agar may help the texture. This is a general table and may vary from recipe to recipe. Adjust one tablespoon at a time. Rice and Corn are the only traditional gluten-free grains. 1/2 cup Ground Nuts may be substituted for 1/2 cup on any of the above grains. Make your own "custom blend" using several grains and starches.

WHEAT PASTA: Pasta is made from many non-wheat grains, look for brown rice, bean threads (made from mung beans), 100% buckwheat soba, spelt and kamut (a non-hybrid wheat tolerated by some with sensitivities), quinoa and corn blend, rice sticks. Try spaghetti squash or zucchini spirals for a more alkaline choice. In restaurants ask for plain rice as a pasta substitution or extra vegetables.

WHITE SAUCE: Parsnips, cauliflower, soft yellow squash or great northern beans. Choose veggie of choice, cook till tender in a pure water source, place in blender, adding just enough of the reserved water to process, continue to add water until desired consistency is reached. Uses vary. From mock mashed potatoes, to creamy soups, to delectable sauces. A tablespoon or two of oil mixed in just before serving will add to the creaminess and flavor. Be creative!

Natural Resources

The following list is from the Coop Directory Service, an online source of information about natural food co-ops. Please note that the Coop Directory Service is a web-based service. They ask that you go to the site first for questions. One of their most common responses to emails is "everything we know and you need are found on our site" www.coopdirectory.org, E-mail address: thegang@coopdirectory.org, Coop Directory Service, 1254 Etna Street, St. Paul, MN 55106, Phone and Fax: 651-774-9189.

Most of these distributors (except the herb companies) carry the following items: groceries (stuff in cans, bottles and boxes), bulk food (large bags of grains, etc.), produce, dairy, frozen food, supplements and personal care products.

If you contact any co-op or warehouse you find here, please tell them that the Co-op Directory Service referred you to them.

Note that only three distributors listed below are strictly co-ops owned by their customers (Ozark, Frontier and Shop Natural, Tucson) - the others are private companies.

NATURAL FOOD COOPERATIVE DISTRIBUTORS

Atlantic Spice Company 1-800-316-7965
Services the area east of the Mississippi with herbs, spices, tea, aromatherapy items, baking, and food items
On line BC ordering? YES
Minimum BC order? $30
Individual retail on-line-sales? YES

Blooming Prairie 1-800-323-2131, ext. 1157
Service area: IA, IL, IN, KS, MI, MN, MO, NE, ND, OH, SD, WI, WY
Service area map? YES
Locate existing BC's or starting new ones YES
On-line BC ordering? YES
Minimum BC order varies depending on your location
Individual retail on-line sales? NO

Co-op America, 1-800-58-GREEN
1612 K Street NW, Suite 600, Washington, DC 20006.
Web: www.coopamerica.com.
For a nominal fee, membership in this organization can put you in touch with other groups, services and products safe for our planet and its people.

Frontier Natural Products Co-op 1-800-786-1388
Serves the nation with herbs, spices, organic coffee, and aromatherapy products
Retail mail order? YES (no minimum order size)
On-line BC ordering? YES
Minimum BC order $75 (smaller order $5 s/h)
Membership application? YES
Individual retail on-line sales? YES

Ozark Coop Warehouse 1-800-967-2667
Service area: AL, AR, FL, GA, KS, LA, MO, MS, OK, Western TN, TX
Locate existing BC's YES
On-line BC ordering? YES
Minimum BC order? $300 -$500
Individual retail on-line sales? N0 (UPS on some items)

Rainbow Natural Foods 1-800-264-7633
Service Area: AR, CO, some IN, some IL, IA, KA, MO, NE, NM, some MI, OK, SD, TX, UT, some WI, WY

Roots & Fruits Cooperative (http://www.rootsproduce.com/) 1-877-241-3030
Service Area: MN, WI, IL, IA, OH, MI, IN
On-line BC ordering: Yes
Minimum BC Order: $650.00
Membership application: No
Individual retail on-line sales: No

San Francisco Herb Company 1-800-227-4530
Services the area west of the Mississippi with herbs, spices, tea, aromatherapy items, baking, and food items
On line BC ordering? YES
Minimum BC order? $30
Individual retail on-line-sales? Yes

ShopNatural Cooperative 1-800-350-2667
Service area: AZ, Southern CA, CO, NM, NV, Western TX, UT
Service area map? YES
Locate existing BC's? YES
On-line BC ordering? YES
Minimum BC Order $250
Individual retail on-line sales? YES

UNFI Eastern Region 1-800-451-4520
Service area: CT, DE, DC (Wash), MA, ME, MD, NH, NJ, NY, RI, VA, VT, Northern GA, Eastern IN, KY, NC, OH, PA, SC, TN, W

UNFI Western Region: Mountain People's Warehouse 1-800-679-6733
Service Area: AL, AZ, CA, HI, ID, MT, NV, OR, UT, WA

United Buying Clubs 1-800-451-2525, ext. 2245
Service area: CT, DE, DC (Wash), MA, ME, MD, NH, NJ, NY, RI, VA, VT, Northern GA, Eastern IN, KY, NC, OH, PA, SC, TN, WV

WHOLESALERS & RETAILERS

- **Allens Naturally,** P.O. Box 514, Farmington MI 48332-0514, Phone: **1-800-352-8971,** Web: www.allensnaturally.com. Safe Cleaning supplies, automatic dishwasher detergent, no animal testing.

- **Allergy Asthma Technology,** 8224 Lehigh Ave., Morton Grove, IL 60053. Phone: **1-800-621-5545,** in Illinois **1-847-966-2952,** Fax: 1-847-966-3068, Web: www.allergyastmatech.com. With a Physician's certificate of medical necessity, purchases from this company may be covered by insurance or as a tax deduction. Vacuum cleaners, bedding, mold remover, etc.

- **Bob's Red Mill, Natural Foods Inc.,** ⓖⒻ 5209 SE International Way, Milwaukie, Oregon 97222, Phone: **1-800-349-2173,** Web: www.bobsredmill.com. Millers of Natural foods, call for their catalog.

- **Cascadian Farm Inc.,** General Mills, Inc., P.O. Box 9452, Minneapolis, MN 55440, Phone: **1-800-624-4123,** Web: www.cascadianfarm.com. Organic fruit sorbet and spreads, juice concentrates, frozen fruits and vegetables.

- **Decent Exposures,** 12554 Lake City Way NE, Seattle, WA 98125, Phone: **1-800-524-4949** or **1-206-364-4540** in Seattle or over seas, Web: www.decentexposures.com. Catalog, 100% cotton undergarments designed by women for women.

- **Dietary Specialities, Inc.,** ⓖⒻ 10 Leslie Court, Whippany, NJ 07981, Phone: **1-888-640-2800,** Web:www.dietspec.com. Pasta, flours, cookies, mixes, crackers, ingredients and condiments.

- **Ener-G Foods, Inc.,** ⓖⒻ 5960 First Avenue South, P.O. Box 84487, Seattle, Washington 98124-5787, Phone: **1-800-331-5222** or **1-206-767-6660,** Web: www.ener-g.com. For breads (yeast-free brown rice bread) brown rice pasta and other supplies for a restricted diet.

- **Food For Life Baking Company Inc.,** ⓖⒻ P.O. Box 1434, Corona, CA 92878, Phone: **1-800-797-5090** or **1-951-279-5090,** Web: www.food-for-life.com. Wheat and Gluten-Free breads and pasta.

- **Frontier Natural Products Co-op,** P.O. Box 299, 3021 78th Street, Norway, IA 52318, Phone: **1-800-669-3275,** Web: www.frontiercoop.com. Non-irradiated herbs and spices, also arrowroot. Call for catalog,

- **Gaiam Inc.,** 360 Interlocken Boulevard, Suite 300, Broomfield, CO 80021, Phone: **1-877-989-6321,** Web: www.gaiam.com. Products in harmony with the Earth.

ⓖⒻ - *notes gluten-free products available*

- **Garnet Hill,** 231 Main Street, Franconia, NH 03580, Phone: **1-800-870-3513,** Web: www.garnethill.com. The Original Natural Fibers Catalog.

- **Gluten-Free Mall,** ⓖ 4927 Sonoma Hwy., Ste C1, Santa Rosa, CA 95409 Phone: **707-509-4528,** Fax: 707-324-6060, Web: www.glutenfreemall.com. Gluten-Free Mall® has the best prices and selection of gluten-free, wheat-free, casein-free and other allergy-related health foods and special dietary products on the Internet!

- **Gluten Solutions, Inc.,** ⓖ 8750 Concourse Court, San Diego, CA 92123, Phone: **1-888-845-8836,** Web: www.GlutenSolutions.com, e-mail: info@glutensolutions.com. The tasteful way to eat healthy for life. A store that carries and will ship a variety of products.

- **Janice's LLC,** 30 Arbor Street South, Hartford, CT 06106, Phone: **1-800-526-4237,** Fax 1-860-523-4178, Web: www.janices.com. Mattresses, bedding, cloth products and a good selection of products for environmentally sensitive individuals.

- **Jason Natural Products Consumer Relations,** The Hain Celestial Group, Inc., 4600 Sleepytime Dr., Boulder, CO 80301, Phone: **1-800-434-4246,** Web: www.jason-natural.com. JASON Natural Personal Care products are available at your local natural / health food stores in United States, Canada and are available around the world. If you are unable to find a particular product, please call the JASON Consumer Hotline: 1-877-JASON-01 (1-877-527-6601).

- **Light for Health,** 101 Eagle Canyon Circle, P.O. Box 1760, Lyons, CO 80540, Phone: **1-800-468-1104,** Web: www.lightforhealth.com. All types of full spectrum lights.

- **Lundberg Family Farms,** ⓖ 5370 Church Street, Richvale, CA 95974, Phone: **1-530-882-4500,** Web: www.lundberg.com. Nutra Farmed Brown Rice Syrup, gluten-free (less than 1% fungal enzymes are used). Quality rice and rice products.

- **Menominee Paper,** 144 First Street, Menominee, MI 49858, Phone: **1-800-258-3781,** Fax: 1-906-864-3284, Web: www. cellutissue.com/orderproducts.php. Natural wax paper by the roll or choose wax paper bags in place of plastic.

- **Mia Bambini Inc.,** 360 Merrimack Street, Riverwalk Building, Lawrence, MA 01843, Phone: **1-800-766-1254** or **1-978-682-3600,** Fax: 1-978-682-3131, Web: www.miabambini.com. Natural garments for children because children should LIVE life to it's fullest, LOVE unconditionally, LAUGH one hundred times a day and follow their DREAMS.

ⓖ *- notes gluten-free products available*

- **NewPage Productions,** Ⓖ Inc., 1910 S. Highland Avenue - Suite 250, Lombard, Illinois 60148, Phone: **1-630-355-7746,** Fax: 1-630-355-7926, Web: www.feelgoodfood.com, email: deborah@feelgoodfood.com. Web site has a secure on-line store featuring The **Home Test pH Kit** along with many healthy products. Site has lots of information, on-line catalog or phone for a catalog. Books, Stevia, Xylitol, cleaning supplies, Goji berries, Green drinks, Pau d'Arco, Yerba Maté, Teeccino, and more.

- **Pacific Foods of Oregon, Inc.,** Ⓖ 19480 SW 97th Avenue, Tualatin, OR 97062, Phone: **1-503-692-9666,** Fax: 503-692-9610, Web: www.pacificfoods.com. Non dairy rice and soy beverages. Rice milk is gluten-free, other products may not be... ask first. They do not sell direct but can give a store by you.

- **Quick D-Frost Tray,** Difficult to find. Try www.ebay.com, defrosting tray.

- **Real Goods Store,** 13771 S. Highway 101, Hopland, CA 95449, Web: www.realgoods.com. Shop online or for a catalog call **1-800-919-2400.** Earth friendly products, specialty solar living.

- **Special Foods,** Ⓖ 9207 Shotgun Ct., Springfield, VA 22153, Phone: **1-703-644-0991,** Fax: 1-703-644-1006, Web: www.specialfoods.com. Alternative flours and pre-made baked goods including white sweet potato, true arrowroot flour, malanga etc. Call or visit web site for catalog.

- **The Gluten-Free Pantry,** Ⓖ P.O Box 840, Glastonbury, CT 06033, Phone: **1-860-633-3826,** Web: www.glutenfree.com. Helping people live well without Gluten. Delicious, easy versatile baking mixes.

- **The Hain Celestial Group,** Consumer Relations, 4600 Sleepytime Dr., Boulder, CO 80301, Phone: **1-800-434-4246,** Web: www.hainpurefoods.com. Maker of expeller pressed oils, non-hydrogenated shortening and other healthy foods.

- **The Natural Choice, Eco Design Co.,** 1365 Rufina Circle, Santa Fe, NM 87505, Phone: **1-800-621-2591,** Fax: 1-860-633-6853, Web: www.bioshieldpaint.com. Catalog of healthy home products, such as safe paint.

- **The Really Great Food Co.,** Ⓖ P.O Box 2239, St. James, NY 11780, Phone: **1-631-361-3553,** Fax 1-631-361-6920, Web: www.reallygreatfoods.com. Exclusively Gluten-Free, Wheat-Free products featuring over a dozen mixes

- **Tinkyáda®,** Ⓖ **Rice Pasta,** Consumer Relations, 4600 Sleepytime Dr., Boulder, CO 80301, Phone: **1-416-609-0016,** Fax: 1-416-609-1316, Web site has recipes: www.tinkyada.com, email: jojo@tinkyada.com, for a store near you. May be found in many grocery stores and natural markets. This company does not sell directly to consumer. Tinkyada is my pick for wheat and gluten-free pasta.

Ⓖ *- notes gluten-free products available*

Natural Resources

- **Van's International Foods, ⓖⒻ** 20318 Gramercy Place, Torrance, CA 90501, Phone: **1-310-320-8611,** Fax: 310-320-8805, Web: www.vansintl.com, email: customerservice@vansintl.com. Toaster waffles gluten-free, yeast-free, wheat-free, egg-free, and dairy-free. They do not have an on-line store, but can give you the name of a store near you who carries their products.

- **ZRT Laboratory,** 1815 NW 169th Pl. Suite 5050, Beaverton, Oregon 97006, Phone: **1-503-466-2445,** Fax: 1-503-466-1636, e-mail: info@zrtlab.com, Web: www.salivatest.com, Hormone Hotline: 1-503-466-9166. The Hormone Hotline is a 24 hour taped audio-library with a growing list of topics on every aspect of hormone balance and testing. This is the place for bio-identical hormones.

Many of these companies offer creative recipes and ideas, please take advantage of what they have to offer. Discover new "safe" retailers not on the list — life is to savor!

ⒼⒻ - *notes gluten-free products available*

Reading List

The articles and books and people who have helped me along the way have been too many to list however, the following list of publications should get you started. These books can all be found: www.feelgoodfood.com or call for a catalog 1-630-355-7746.

A.D.D. The Natural Approach 40 pages. Help for children with Attention Deficit Disorder and Hyperactivity. - paperback, by Nina Anderson and Howard Peiper, revised edition.

Anatomy of the Spirit 300 pages. The Seven Stages of Power and Healing - paperback, by Caroline Myss, PH.D.

Arthritis, Childers' Diet That Stops It! 238 pages. The nightshades, ill health, aging and shorter life. Filled with science and evidence to avoid this food group.

Colon Health 118 pages. The key to a vibrant life! - paperback, by Norman W. Walker, D.Sc., Ph.D.

Cooking Healthy Gluten and Casein-Free Food for Children by Betsy Prohaska

Digestive Enzymes 30 pages. The key to good health and longevity - paperback, by Rita Elkins, M.H.

Don't Drink Your Milk 113 pages. New frightening medical facts about the world's most overrated nutrient. - paperback, by Frank A. Oski, M.D.

Essential Fatty Acids 32 pages. "Good" fats that protect the cardiovascular system and promote overall health. - paperback, by Deborah Lee

Fats that Heal Fats that Kill 456 pages. How eating the right fats and oils improves energy, fat loss, immune function, longevity and more.

Fibromyalgia - A Nutritional Approach 30 pages. A comprehensive guide to combating the complex syndrome of fibromyalgia. - paperback, by William Hennen, Ph. D.

Food Additives 80 pages. A shopper's guide to what's safe and what's not, revised edition. A pocket book. - paperback, by Christine Hoza Farlow, D.C.,

Food & Behavior 220 pages. A natural connection. - paperback, by Barbara Reed Stitt, Ph. D.

Food Combining and Digestion 118 pages. 101 ways to improve digestion. - paperback, by Steve Meyerowitz, "Sproutman"

Food Combining Made Easy 63 pages, paperback, by Herbert M. Shelton

Fresh Vegetable and Fruit Juices 118 pages. What's missing in your body? Enlarged - revised edition - paperback, by Norman W. Walker, D.Sc., Ph.D.

Reading List

From Here To Longevity 375 pages. Your complete guide for a long and healthy life. - paperback, by Mitra Ray, Ph.D., with Patricia Cannon Childs and Cynthia Sholes, Ph.D., Science Editor

Gluten-Free 101, easy basic dishes without wheat over 149 pages. With charts, substitutions, and variations - paperback, by Carol Fenster, Ph.D.

Gluten Intolerance 26 pages. A Keats good health guide. A little book with big information - by Beatrice Trum Hunter

Healthy Healing - 12th edition over 650 pages. A Guide to self-healing for everyone. - paperback, by Linda Page, Ph.D., Traditional Naturopath

Home Test pH Kit Booklet 32 pages. A guide to understanding your body's pH. - by Deborah Page Johnson, B.F.A.

How to Prevent and Treat Cancer with Natural Medicine 415 pages. A natural arsenal of diabetes-fighting tools for prevention and treatment, and coping with side effects. - paperback, by Dr. Michael Murray, Dr. Tim Birdsall, Dr. Joseph E. Pizzorno, Dr. Paul Reilly

How to Prevent and Treat Diabetes with Natural Medicine 369 pages. A natural arsenal of diabetes-fighting tools for prevention and treatment designed to boost the effectiveness of conventional therapies. - paperback, by Michael Murray, N.D. and Michael Lyon, M.D.

Juicing for Life 350 pages. A guide to the health benefits of fresh fruit and vegetable juicing. - paperback, by Cherie Calbom and Maureen Keane

Living Well Without Wheat The Gluten-Free Gourmet over 330 pages, with charts, substitutions, and variations - paperback, by Bette Hagman

Natural Cures - "They Don't Want You To Know About" 570 pages - paperback, by Kevin Trudeau

Nature's Sweetener Stevia 29 pages. Sweeten your health and life with stevia. - paperback, by Rita Elkins, M.H.

Nutritional Guidelines for Correcting Behavior 60 pages. Handbook on nutritional counseling for parents, teachers, counselors, psychologists, social workers and correctional personnel. - paperback, by Barbara Reed Stitt, Ph. D.

Stevia, Naturally Sweet Recipes 213 pages. Naturally sweet recipes for desserts, drinks and more! - paperback, by Rita DePuydt

The Battle for Health is Over pH over 115 pages. Alkaline vs. acid....The pH scale, life and death hangs in the balance. - paperback, by Gary Tunsky, with interview from Crusader Magazine editor Greg Ciola

The Candida - Yeast Syndrome 48 pages. A Keats good health guide. A little book with big information - by Ray C. Wunderlich, Jr., M.D.

The Coconut Oil Miracle 239 pages. Previously published as The Healing Miracles of Coconut Oil - paperback, by Bruce Fife, C.N., N.D., forward by, Jon J. Kabara, Ph.D.

The Complete Book of Essential Oils & Aromatherapy over 420 pages. Over 600 natural, non-toxic & fragrant recipes to create health, beauty and a safe home environment. - paperback, by Valerie Ann Worwood

The Complete Guide to Wheat-Free Cooking 358 pages, paperback, by Phyllis Potts

The Fat Flush Foods 150 pages. The world's best foods, seasonings, and supplements to flush the fat from every body. - paperback, by Ann Louise Gittleman, M.S., C.N.S.

The Hidden Messages in Water more than 160 pages plus color pictures - paperback, by Masaru Emoto

The Little Book of Bleeps over 80 pages. Color photos and quotations from the movie... What tHe BLeeP Do wE (k)now!? - paperback

The Liver Cleansing Diet over 185 pages. A life-saving breakthrough for men and women. - paperback, by Dr. Sandra Cabot

The Miracle of Fasting over 250 pages. Detox body - recharge health. - paperback, by Paul C. Bragg, N.D., Ph.D, life extension specialist. and Patricia Bragg, N.D., Ph.D., health and fitness expert

The Miracle of Stevia over 278 pages. Discover the healing power of nature's herbal sweetener. - paperback, by James A. May

The pH Miracle 334 pages. Balance your diet, reclaim your health. - paperback, by Robert O. Young, Ph.D., and Shelley Redford Young, foreword Jane Clayson, co-anchor, The Early Show

The pH Miracle for Diabetes over 333 pages. The revolutionary diet plan for type 1 and type 2 diabetics. - hard bound, by Robert O. Young, Ph.D., and Shelley Redford Young

The pH Miracle for Weight Loss 373 pages. Balance Your Body Chemistry, Achieve Your Ideal Weight - paperback, by Robert O. Young and Shelley Redford Young

The Sexy Years 357 pages. Discover the Hormone Connection: The Secret to Fabulous Sex, Great Health, and Vitality, For Women and Men - paperback, by Suzanne Somers

Reading List

The Stevia Cookbook over 172 pages. Cooking with nature's calorie-free sweetener. - paperback, by Ray Sahelian, M.D., and Donna Gates

The Sweet Miracle of Xylitol over 84 pages. Cooking with nature's calorie-free sweetener. - paperback, by Fran Gare, N.D., research Reesa Sokoloff, M.S., R.D.

The Truth About Beauty more than 360 pages with easy how-to charts and lists - paperback, by Kat James

Prescription for Dietary Wellness - 2nd edition over 775 pages. All new, completely revised and updated. Over 100,00 copies in print. - paperback, by Phyllis A. Balch, CNC

Prescription for Natural Cures 724 pages. With charts and highlighted information - paperback, by James F. Balch, M.D. and Mark Stengler, N.D.

Prescription for Nutritional Healing - 3rd edition over 775 pages. America's #1 guide to natural health, completely revised and expanded. - paperback, by Phyllis A. Balch, CNC

Prescription for Nutritional Healing - A-to-Z Guide to Supplements over 285 pages. Portions previously published in part one of Prescription for Nutritional Healing. - paperback, by Phyllis A. Balch, CNC

RAW - The UNcook Book over 285 pages. Beautiful full color and hard bound. New vegetarian food for life - by Juliano, with Erika Lenkert

Rawsome! over 350 pages, and 200 recipes. Maximizing health, energy, and culinary delight with the Raw Foods Diet. - paperback, by Brigitte Mars

Sick & Tired? 300 pages. Reclaim Your Inner Terrain. - paperback, by Robert O. Young, Ph.D., D.Sc., with Shelley Redford Young, L.M.T.

Suzanne Somers' Slim & Sexy Forever 316 pages - Foreword by David R. Allen, M.D. - hardcover, by Suzanne Somers

Vaccines 126 pages. Are they really safe & effective? New updated and revised edition Over 100.000 copies sold. - paperback, by Neil Z. Miller, forewords by, George R. Schwartz, M.D. and Harold E. Buttram, M.D.

Water - The Ultimate Cure 89 pages . Discover why water is the most important ingredient in your diet and find out which water is right for you. - paperback, by Steve Meyerowitz

Your Body's Many Cries for Water 188 pages. You Are Not Sick, You Are Thirsty! Don't Treat Thirst With Medications - paperback, by F. Batmanghelidj, M.D.

Is The Staff Of Life
Beating You Over The Head?

For most of us it is impossible to imagine life without wheat. After all, isn't wheat the cornerstone of good health? Not for everyone, in fact, not for most. I believe that just because a problem has not been diagnosed does not make it any less real.

When we published the first edition of The Feel Good Food Guide I had no idea how widespread the sensitivities toward wheat were. There is not just one cause and there is no real cure, other than abstinence. Now, you are really depressed! Don't be, you are not alone and there is life without wheat.

When hosting a Cooking Class there is always at least one person in the audience who is faced with gluten intolerance or celiac sprue. Celiac disease is an inflammatory condition of the small intestine. The disease is genetic, however, symptoms are only brought on by the ingestion of gluten and in some cases casein, the protein in dairy products.

Most commonly the disease is diagnosed around age two when wheat is introduced into the diet. However, celiac disease can begin any time in life, it all depends on how much of the intestine is involved. The wheat protein gluten triggers an inflammatory reaction in the small bowel which results in a decrease in the amount of surface area available for nutrient, fluid, and electrolyte absorption. Be grateful if you have easily recognizable symptoms, undetected the disease could lead to more serious health problems including cancer.

In other words if you have celiac sprue and continue to eat gluten of any kind in any amount your intestines will not be able to absorb nutrients. Even though you may be eating a healthy diet and living a healthy lifestyle, your body may genetically not be able to benefit. Intestinal villi become "glued" down and can not do their job.

Different food factors beyond celiac disease may make wheat unsuitable for other individuals as well, such as the incompatibility of blood lectins and food lectins. According to some researchers over 80% of the population may be sensitive to the lectins in wheat. Then there is the candida issue, the opportunist organism that can cause symptoms ranging from chronic fatigue to PMS and brain fog. Candida thrives on over processed refined flour, sugar and yeast, many such unhealthy foods containing wheat are eaten daily by most Americans. Gluten has also been associated with symptoms from Autism to ADD. These are but a few of the concerns regarding wheat consumption.

If you have eliminated wheat and have given some of the alternative gluten grains used in this book a try and are still having a problem it may be the gluten part of the grain. For a list of gluten grains see Food Families Section page 10 and By Any Other Name page 18.

For conversion information and alternative flours see page 185.

Gluten-Free Living

Celiac disease is defined as the body's inability to metabolize gluten due to an enzyme deficiency. Gluten is a protein found in many grains. The most common source today is wheat flour. Other common gluten grains are oat, barley and rye. When the body is stressed by the gluten it may present with the following symptoms; bloating, with a distended abdomen, gas, 3-6 poorly formed, foul smelling stools per day, diarrhea and slow growth. An additional symptom is a bluish-red stripe that starts at the inside corner of the nose that runs below the eye and extends downward and outward.

Symptoms of celiac disease vary because the amount of surface area affected may vary. Severe symptoms such as diarrhea, weakness, and weight loss may indicate a marked decrease in intestinal absorptive surfaces. On the other hand, other symptoms could be anemia related fatigue and have no symptoms referable to the gastrointestinal tract. Some long term problems related to the disease may include osteogenic bone disease, tetany and rare neurologic disorders.

Gluten sensitivity can also manifest itself as a blistering, burning, itchy rash on the extensor surface of the body.

Because barley malt is used in manufacturing of most rice beverages and not added to the final product, the F.D.A. does not require it be listed on the label. Therefore it is possible to get a reaction even though rice is the only grain listed as an ingredient on the label (barley is a gluten grain).

Even if symptoms are not severe, there are two reasons to avoid gluten with a gluten-free diet:

1. A subgroup of these patients will progress to more severe disease and develop more symptoms and . . .

2. There is an increased incidence of small intestinal lymphomas and adenocarcinomas in individuals with celiac disease.

Celiac disease runs in families and is genetic. First generation relatives of individuals with celiac disease may or may not manifest symptoms of the disease. Predisposition to gluten sensitivity has been mapped to the major histocompatibility (MHC) D region on chromosome 6.

Gluten-free grains and products may be found in our "Natural Resources" section pages 186-192. Gluten-free sources will have a **GF** next to their name.

The Three C's of Gluten-Free Baking are:

1. **Content:** Choose gluten-free food items, not gluten-restricted.

2. **Contact:** Use clean tools for cutting, mixing and serving. Clean cooking/grilling/griddle surfaces. Consider buying duplicate equipment for hard-to-clean items such as toasters.

3. **Contamination:** Develop gluten-free kitchen habits, storage plans and procedures for mixing and cooking and baking to avoid cross contamination with gluten-containing foods.

Call the manufacturer to be sure that they are following the 3 C's as well!

Ingredients to enhance gluten-free baking: Agar Agar, Xanthan gum, Baking Soda, Baking powder (has a short shelf life), unflavored Gelatin, naturally acidic ingredients such as Vitamin C Crystals mixed with Baking Soda allow baked goods to rise.

Flours/starches that mix well with Brown rice flour are Tapioca, Potato, Arrowroot, Sweet Potato. Flours made from Legumes, Beans, Nuts and Seeds also enhance home-made baking mixes, check out Special Foods (page 191).

The following patient organizations provide information on celiac disease, gluten sensitivity and dietary treatment:

American Celiac Society / Dietary Support Coalition. Also supports dermatitis herpetiformis, Crohn's disease, lactose intolerance, & other food allergies. WRITE: American Celiac Society, c/o Annette Bentley, P.O.Box 23455, New Orleans, LA 70183-0455, CALL: **1-504-737-3293** Annette Bentley, E-MAIL: amerceliacsoc@yahoo.net, WEBSITE: http://www.americanceliacsociety.org

Celiac Disease Foundation. Information is also available in Spanish. WRITE: Celiac Disease Foundation, 13251 Ventura Blvd., Suite 1, Studio City, CA 91604, CALL: **1-818-990-2354** (day), FAX: 1-818-990-2379, E-MAIL: cdf@celiac.org, WEBSITE: http://celiac.org

Celiac Sprue Association/United States of America, Inc. Offers group development guidelines. WRITE: Celiac Sprue Assn. USA, P.O. Box 31700, Omaha, NE 68131, CALL: **1-877-272-4272** or 402-558-0600, FAX: 402-558-1347, E-MAIL: celiacs@csaceliacs.org, WEBSITE: http://www.csaceliacs.org

If you think you or a family member may have celiac disease contact your doctor to arrange for appropriate testing.

Feingold Association of the United States. Dedicated to helping children and adults apply proven dietary techniques for better behavior, learning and health. It is a non-profit public charity. WRITE: Feingold Association of the United State, 554 East Main Street Suite 301, Riverhead, NY 11901, CALL: **1-631-369-9340** (Eastern Time), FAX: 1-631-369-2988, EMAIL: help@feingold.org, WEBSITE: http://www.feingold.org

Gluten Intolerance Group of North America. Mission is to increase awareness by providing accurate and up to date information. WRITE: Gluten Intolerance Group, 15110 10 Ave. SW, Suite A, Seattle, WA 98166-1820, CALL: **1-206-246-6652,** FAX: 1-206-246-6531, E-MAIL: info@gluten.net, WEBSITE: http://www.gluten.net

Living Without. Magazine whos primary aim is to support and educate readers with allergies and food and/or chemical sensitivities. WRITE: Living Without, P.O. Box 2126, Northbrook, IL 60065, CALL: **1-847-480-8810,** EMAIL: Marketing@LivingWithout.com, WEBSITE: http://www.livingwithout.com

Pathways Medical Advocates. Specialize in dietary interventions and integrative treatments. WRITE: Pathways Medical Advocates, 5411 Hwy 50, Delavan, WI 53115, CALL: **1-262-740-3000**, FAX: 1-262-740-3001, EMAIL: missy@pathwaysmed.com, WEBSITE: http://www.pathwaysmed.com

The Food Allergy & Anaphylaxis Network. FAAN serves as the communication link between the patient and others. WRITE: The Food Allergy & Anaphylaxis Network, 11781 Lee Jackson Hwy., Suite 160, Fairfax, VA 22033-3309, CALL: **1-800-929-4040,** FAX: 1-703-691-2713, EMAIL: faan@foodallergy.org, WEBSITE: www.foodallergy.org

Just like gluten, the protein in grains can cause digestive problems in people. So can Casein, the protein in dairy and most non-dairy cheeses. The same foods and items that may cause a candida flair-up may also create a problem for people with gluten intolerance. If you are not sure, call the manufacturer to find out if their product is truly gluten-free. Never assume. Remember even trace amounts may be enough to create a non-absorbing environment in your gut. Once again . . . READ ALL LABELS! It's o-kay to question anything going into your body or affecting your health.

As I mentioned earlier, the elimination of gluten and casein helps people suffering from Celiac Sprue. The elimination of these two foods may also help with everything from ADD/ADHD to Autism and other unrelated health complaints. Organizations, publications and clinics which may offer some new ideas on how to help are listed above.

For Me To Be Healthier I Am Waiting For...

1. Inspiration
2. Permission
3. Reassurance
4. The Herb Tea To Be Ready
5. My Turn
6. Someone To Smooth The Way
7. The Rest Of The Rules
8. Someone To Change
9. More Time
10. A Disaster
11. Time To Almost Run Out
12. The Kids To Leave Home
13. A Better Time
14. A More Favorable Horoscope
15. The Two-Minute Warning
16. Tomorrow
17. The Stakes To Be Higher
18. My Way To Be Clear
19. The Things I Don't Understand Or Approve Of To Go Away
20. Clearly Written Set of Instructions
21. You To Go First
22. A Cue Card
23. My Smoking Urges To Subside
24. A Less Turbulent time
25. Morning
26. My Doctor's Approval, My Father's Permission, My Minister's Blessing Or My Lawyer's O-Kay
27. Next Season
28. A Signal From Heaven
29. Spring
30. An End To Poverty, Injustice Cruelty, Deceit, Incompetence Petulance, Crime And Offensive Suggestions

Don't Wait

Variety. Moderation. Consistency.
Eat Smart. Be Healthy. Start Today!

Making the Connection

Because of the Home Test pH Kit, we receive a lot of phone calls from people with questions concerning pH levels and proper use of the kit. I have noticed a "hit" list of common foods that people eat on a daily basis that seem harmless enough, yet are holding their health prisoner. So to address this reoccurring theme and to acknowledge the power of addictive foods I am going to list some common "thought-to-be-healthy" foods and habits. In addition to these foods being common allergic foods these foods are also highly acid-forming. Eating these foods on a daily basis will never allow the body to do any type of real repair. Body functions that should be repairing are spending all of their time doing clean-up and damage control. After a while an exhausted body starts to become unable to even do the basics required for good health.

PEANUT BUTTER - Thought by most to be a healthy protein source. If you are buying commercial peanut butter you are also getting hydrogenated or partially hydrogenated oil (these are trans fats, no amount is alright) and sugar. All peanuts (even organic) may contain up to 26 different types of fungus. The government even has strict regulations on aflatoxin. Aflatoxin is a naturally occurring substance produced by a mold that can grow on peanuts and is a concern for manufactures. Peanut products must constantly be tested to adhere to these government regulations. The same mold information goes for corn and corn products.

OATMEAL, BANANAS AND MILK - Starting your day with this highly acid meal makes catch-up the name of the game for the rest of the day. Milk that has been homogenized and pasteurized, made from cows that have been fed hormones, antibiotics and unnatural foods, is poison to your body. Milking machines in factory farms can cause blood and puss to go into the milk. Milk also turns to sugar rapidly in your body making it highly acid-forming. Because of the high protein content of milk, calcium becomes mostly unabsorbable (even the calcium from other food sources). Bananas are one of the most high glycemic foods available and prone to mold. If you are worried about potassium, eat some fresh spinach, a half cup of spinach has about the same potassium content as a banana. Oatmeal was once only used for live stock feed. Oatmeal has gluten and is highly acidic. Yes, it has heart healthy fiber but so does that half cup of spinach. Eat organic oatmeal or flour later in the day with vegetables.

CHEESE - Oh the power of cheese! All of the statements made above about milk apply here - only to the tenth power. Highly concentrated amounts of casomorphine found in casein is why so many people can not give up cheese. Casomorphine has one tenth the same addictive properties of morphine. No wonder people can't give up this highly addictive acid food.

YOGURT - Yes, in a perfect world, yogurt made from raw organic milk with all of the acidophilus cultures in tact would add beneficial bacteria to the gut. However, by law, yogurt must be pasteurized, this heating process kills all of the natural acidophilus cultures. Plus, all of the statements made above about milk apply here as well.

COFFEE - An 8 ounce cup of coffee contains 200 mg. of caffeine. This highly acid-forming beverage (about 4.2 pH depending on the roast) claims to give a boost to the day. What it really does is artificially stimulate with caffeine (the chemicals used to make decaf are equally acid-forming). It's no mystery that most people who start the day with coffee also suffer from heartburn. "Only one-cup-a-day" is enough to keep body systems acid all day long, no matter how many salads are eaten. Want to wake up in the morning and have balanced energy all day long, try a Green Smoothie pages 46-47.

If we drink **"SODA ONCE-IN-A-WHILE"** - Do the math. It takes 32 eight ounce glasses of alkaline water to neutralize one eight ounce glass of cola. All soda is acid forming. They either contain artificial sugar or high fructose corn sweetener which are both acid-forming. They all are carbonated which is carbonic acid. Most have citric acid and the phosphoric acid found in cola is a known cause of osteoporosis. Because of the high acid load of soda, our body uses more water to process the soda than the liquid in the soda itself. Soda actually causes dehydration, making us thirsty and wanting more.

Other foods that are not a good idea: **RAISINS**, because of the mold potential and high sugar content; **SOY MILK**, contains sugar, is acid-forming and is not a good idea especially if not organic; **FRUIT AFTER OR WITH MEALS**, this food combining nightmare causes the fruit to ferment before nutrients can be absorbed by the intestines; **BAGEL AND CREAM CHEESE**, will cause a brief sugar high followed by fatigue and is highly acid-forming; **ANYTHING WHITE**, white rice, white bread, white potato, banana, refined sugar, dairy, hydrogenated shortening, etc. These are all highly acid-forming, highly suspect allergic foods.

LAST BUT NOT LEAST; Refrigerators void of a green lining. People, people, people, we have forgotten the basics. It isn't about what we do, sometimes it's about what we don't do. We can tap dance around this all we want. The bottom line is this - if we eat 4 ounces of chicken we need to eat 16 ounces of something green and leafy to balance the meal. All the knowledge in the world does us no good if we don't put into practice what we have learned. Change is an inside job - that spark of desire within us is what moves mountains. It's inspiration not perspiration that will allow us to make the biggest shift in our reality.

Index & Reference

Index & Reference

Index & Reference